CHRISTENDOM LOST

SIMON LENNON

Christendom Lost
Non-fiction
Christianity, Theology
A book in the collection: The West
A book in the series: Cultures
Published by Pine Hill Books
Copyright © 2016, 2020, 2024 by Simon Lennon.
All rights reserved.
This book or any portion thereof may not be reproduced, stored in or introduced into a retrieval system, or transmitted in any form or by any means whatsoever (electronic, mechanical, photocopying, recording, or otherwise) without the express written prior permission of the author and the publisher, except for the use of brief quotations in a book review, scholarly journal, or student assignment.
The author asserts his moral rights.
ISBN 978-1-925446-04-3 (electronic)
ISBN 978-1-925446-20-3 (paperback)
57,000 words, plus bibliography, references to 60,000 words
Cover image: Saint Saviour's Church, Iandra, 2012

*In memory of Ian Biner,
my trusted friend*

CONTENTS

1. God and Country 1
2. Collective Guilt 9
3. Feeling Unforgiven 17
4. Discrimination 23
5. Postmodern Christianity 30
6. Multicultural Christianity 38
7. God and Jesus 46
8. White Christian Burden 54
9. Belonging 62
10. Other People's Churches 68
11. Church and State 77
12. Economic Religion 84
13. Religion for Sale 92
14. Sport 99
15. Other People's Festivals 105
16. The Religion that Hides 113
17. Our Lands of Other Faiths 120
18. Holy Mothers 128
19. Environmentalism 135
20. Voluntary Human Extinction 142
21. The End of Christendom 148
22. Saving Christendom 157
Bibliography, References 164
About the Author 176

1. GOD AND COUNTRY

The only races to have taken up individualism since World War II weren't just Western. We were Christian. We ceased being Christian peoples not because we ceased being Christian, but because we ceased being peoples.

It was all very well for the Holy Father, Pope Benedict XVI, to want Europeans to rediscover our Christian heritage, but Western peoples of faith are no more embracing of our European heritage. Neither the faithful nor faithless still think of us being Christendom, a collective Christian corpus, as we did until 1914 and, to some degree, until 1939. We're no longer Christian for being European peoples, whether in Europe or abroad: the Christian West. We're individually Christian or not.

We won't revive religion for the West (let alone be a light again for the rest of the world) without reviving our collective identities. We won't be Christian peoples again without being peoples again.

Other races remain races, retaining their religions because they retain their cultures. Fijians, for example, are Christian for being Fijian. Christianity is their heritage, if only since the nineteenth century. Defending its parishioners and people as Western churches no longer imagine is the Methodist Church in Fiji, to which most Fijians belong. It described proposals from 2008 to allow all Fijian citizens (including Hindu Indians) to call themselves Fijian as "daylight robbery" of indigenous Fijians. For Fijians and their church, only people racially Fijian are Fijian.

Not us. The Church that once defended Christendom no longer cares.

Western churches still advocate, but not for the people who built our churches or for our religion. They advocate for other races and their religions.

The last week of September 2014, police arrested fifteen Muslims plotting the beheading of people in Sydney and Brisbane. Worried more about Muslims feeling unwelcome than Christians being murdered, Gordon Uniting Church declared from its Pacific

Highway noticeboard: *"Muslims Welcome Here."*

We of the faith are no less responsible than anyone else for the decline of Western Christianity. We help everyone, but when there is a conflict between Western interests and other peoples' aspirations, we favour other peoples. Our only difference with Western peoples without faith is our presumption we act with God's will, as if God too prefers other races and their religions.

Western Christianity is eroding from within. Championing others more than our own we call social justice, but they're other people's societies. We're individuals, with no more thought of our race than those without faith: the injustice of neglecting our own. We've succumbed to a Christian individualism, a Christian multiculturalism purporting to be part of a single world view. Why would people sit in churches more interested in everyone else?

The last Sunday in July 2013, Ben preached at our family's Uniting church. Fellow Australians' anxieties about illegal immigrants (primarily Muslim South Asians) sailing towards Australia to claim asylum, Ben attributed to Australian senses of national borders, sovereignty, and "a kind of country body corpus." He then dismissed those things for being unreal, as only the West does.

They were real until recently. They're more real than ever before for other races.

In the church were copies of the preamble to the Uniting Church in Australia constitution adopted in 2009. Paragraph 2 respected "*Aboriginal and Islander peoples, who continue to understand themselves to be the traditional owners and custodians (meaning 'sovereign' in the languages of the First Peoples) of these lands and waters since time immemorial.*" Paragraph 7 spoke of Aborigines suffering "*dispossession and the denial of their proper place in this land.*"

National borders, sovereignty, and body corpora are as real as we want them to be. If they're unreal for countries, then they're unreal for people. Without collective corpora, we've no families or churches. If national borders and sovereignty aren't real, then private property isn't real, but the books of the Bible defend peoples' territories.

In chapter 25, verses 23 and 24 of the Book of Leviticus, God commands Israelites to retain ultimate control and title to their territory, even if they lease it to others. Verse 25 commands their nearest relatives to buy their property if poverty forces them to sell, failing which they must later buy it back if they can.

The Book of Numbers, chapter 36, verse 8 requires daughters inheriting land to marry within their fathers' clans. At Chapter 23, verses 4 and 5 of the Book of Joshua, Joshua bestowed land to the tribes of Israel as their inheritances. It included land that they conquered.

Both Testaments speak to races and nations. So do we, but not for us. The countries we don't have when they're reason to exclude immigrants, are countries we have when they're reason to admit them. The Sunday after Ben rejected all sense of nationhood, Reverend Laurel claimed Australian government policies to control the arrival of asylum seekers destroyed "the soul of the nation."

Ben acknowledged that Biblical obligations to show mercy don't require self-sacrifice, but we're sacrificing our countries, races, and churches. The Anglican archbishop of Sydney, Peter Jensen, acknowledged in a television interview late in October 2009 that immigration was against the Church's future, without suggesting the Church save itself.

We're Christians without countries. The only selves the West now understands are individual selves.

Christians outside the individualist West don't demand their countries welcome immigrants. Justice and mercy for their forebears, compatriots, and descendants demand they keep outsiders at bay.

That last Sunday in July 2013, a divorced Scotsman at our family's Uniting church dismissed my comparisons in attitudes to asylum seekers between the West and Asia. "We have a different standard," said Craig.

"We think we're superior," I replied.

"Not superior," he said quickly.

"We don't say we're superior to anyone, but that's what it is." Craig never spoke to me again.

Our anti-racial, anti-national West encompasses everyone equally. The Bible doesn't.

The first two verses of the Book of Nehemiah, Chapter 13, describe the Israelites hearing the Book of Moses declare that no Ammonites or Moabites should ever be admitted into the assembly of God, because they had not provided the Israelites with food and water but instead hired Balaam to call a curse upon them. The Israelites respond, at verse 3, by excluding all people of foreign descent.

"Do not hate a fellow Israelite in your heart," God commanded Moses to tell the Israelites at chapter 19, verse 17 of the Book of Leviticus. "Rebuke your neighbour frankly so you will not share in his guilt."

An Israelite's neighbour is a fellow Israelite. The command not to hate is of a fellow Israelite.

Love thy neighbour is a command of kindness to our compatriots, including those we don't know. It's the sense of community underpinning racism, nationalism, and other tribalism.

Jesus' parable of the Good Samaritan demonstrates that our generosity should be to people with whom we disagree. Samaritans were fellow Semites claiming descent from particular Israelite tribes and adherence to a purer, ancient form of their religion than others. Their modern-day equivalents aren't people from other races but, for example, the racists and nationalists we condemn among our own.

The Bible talks of foreigners, thereby affirming races and nations. At a time other religions imposed no obligations to outsiders, the Bible spoke of them. Kindness to foreigners isn't at a people's expense.

The most generous obligation to foreigners is in chapter 19, verse 34 of the Book of Leviticus. It isn't an obligation to admit them, but a consequence of doing so. "*The foreigner residing among you must be treated as your native born. Love them as yourself, for you were foreigners in Egypt.*" It might be another rule specifically for Jews who'd lived so long in Egypt, inapplicable to races without similar histories. It assumes the foreigner does no harm.

People living by Christian faith don't risk harming their own, but may let foreigners use what they can't. In giving out the scraps, chapter 14, verse 21 of the Book of Deuteronomy discriminates between different types of foreigners. "*Do not eat anything you find already dead. You may give it to the foreigner residing in any of your towns, and they may eat it, or you may sell it to any other foreigner.*"

In ancient Hebrew, a foreigner residing in a town was a "*ger.*" One passing through was a "*nokrî.*" Original Hebrew and Greek Biblical texts use several different words for what we broadly call others.

Deuteronomy abounds with discrimination. Chapter 15, verses 1 to 3 requires Israelites to cancel each other's debts once every seven years, but allows them to demand repayment from foreigners.

Morals among a people are inapplicable to outsiders, which can be a problem or a privilege. *"You may charge a foreigner interest, but not a fellow Israelite,"* says Deuteronomy, chapter 23, verse 20, espousing economic nationalism. Charging each other interest separates people economically, but even after refining the rule in the Middle Ages we made a mess of carrying the prohibition into effect. Jews became Europe's moneylenders.

"Deliver me and rescue me from the hands of foreigners whose mouths are full of lies, whose right hands are deceitful," would be xenophobic and racial vilification in our multicultural West. Those words were said, or sung, thousands of years ago by David: God's favourite, in spite of his sins. The words are Psalm 144, verse 11.

In the Book of Jeremiah, chapter 5, verse 19 the punishment for abandoning God is serving foreigners, giving up our countries. (It still is.) *"And when the people ask, 'Why has the Lord our God done all this to us?' you will tell them, 'As you have forsaken me and served foreign gods in your own land, so now you will serve foreigners in a land not your own.'"*

Increasingly since the Second World War, the West has rejected our races, cultures, and God. By the early twenty-first century, many Western Christians are no more interested in Biblical teaching with which they disagree than are those without faith.

The Sunday before the 2010 Australian election, I asked Brother Ned Gerber, an American Swiss at our parish Anglican church (an Anglo-Catholic church), what he thought of the likelihood Australians would elect an unmarried atheist living with her boyfriend as prime minister. (I still liked her.) Joining the discussion over dinner, our South Asian friend Essy was more concerned about the married Liberal Party leader of faith, Tony Abbott, "playing upon people's fears." By that, she meant his promises to stop the boatloads of asylum seekers coming to the country.

Ned saw only the Greens political party as being acceptable for their support for asylum seekers, "even though many of their policies are hostile to Christianity." In the choice between God and immigration, we're pumping for immigration.

"They don't like borders at all," I told Ned.

"We need immigration."

"No, we don't."

"With our birth rates, we need it for economic growth," Ned insisted. "Countries need birth rates of two point one for economic growth," he said, referring to the number of babies born per woman.

Biblical passages like chapter 13, verse 5 of the Epistle to the Hebrews don't keep us from the West's fixation with commercial expansion. *"Keep your lives free from the love of money and be content with what you have."*

"Countries like Korea, Japan, have lower birth rates than ours," I replied to Ned. "They don't have immigration."

"It's not just that," said Essy. "It's population density."

"Vast areas of this country are desert," I told her.

"Even apart from that."

Europe's high population density had not saved Europe from immigration. Essy, her family, and race gained from the West's open borders. Ned, his family, and race did not.

By the time I came across our parish Anglican church treasurer James at the Pymble Ladies College garden party (which was really a fête, but the college called it a garden party), the election was over. We both thought Abbott should cease trying to make favour with the independent parliamentarians who'd fobbed off their conservative constituencies to return the government, but act like the opposition leader they'd compelled him to remain. James went onto say that he cringed to hear Abbott talk of asylum seekers. James wanted their applications for asylum processed in Australia.

Refugees are just another tranche of immigrants. James wanted Australia to admit all comers for no other reason than they showed the character to come, thinking the continent could sustain a hundred and fifty or two hundred million people (overwhelming what had been Christian Australia).

We don't believe in countries in any meaningfully defined way, not for the West. James added, "I'm not very comfortable with what's happening in France."

Making the connection took me a moment. "You mean with the gypsies?"

He did. President Nicholas Sarkozy responded to high crime rates and problems of illegal accommodations by deporting thousands of Roma, although his actions reeked of political posturing. European Union rules allowed citizens of other

European Union countries to turn around past the border and walk back into France.

"I've encountered gypsies," I told James, "in Romania, Hungary, Czechoslovakia, Italy." I shook my head. "I can't really criticise him."

The only times I'd heard much of churches in France were them giving sanctuary to illegal immigrants; separating church and state cut both ways. American churches espouse a wide range of positions, while defying American law and interest to welcome illegal immigrants.

When Western churches speak loudest, we no longer speak for our people. "*We are disgraced,*" says Jeremiah, chapter 51, verse 51, "*for we have been insulted and shame covers our faces, because foreigners have entered the holy places of the Lord's house.*"

When three Vietnamese asylum seekers disappeared while attending St Mary's Cathedral, Darwin in 2011, I was surprised refugees still came from prospering Vietnam. That December, Kiet, a lawyer who'd left Vietnam in the early 1980s but returned there for his honeymoon in 2001 among other trips and holidays, told me they were economic refugees, wanting Australian welfare and wages.

It was easy to imagine Father Paul's complicity in the Vietnamese escape. "Good on 'em," the Roman Catholic priest told immigration department officials. "If I had my way, I'd throw open the doors of the detention centre and say, 'Out you go'."

He'd believed the Vietnamese telling him they were escaping political persecution, but the persecution was pretty paltry. "I think that sometimes to be different from the majority is to show that you're possibly against the government in Vietnam. It becomes a political thing."

The Vietnamese weren't fleeing persecution. They were fleeing a political thing. Gosh, we could all be refugees.

We can hardly expect Muslims, Jews, and people of other religions to put Western countries ahead of their religions when, so often since World War II, we haven't put our countries ahead of our private little religions: our religious individualism. Our parish Anglican church organist Brett earned a Bachelor of Theology degree from Sydney College of Divinity, but listed his religious views on the Facebook website as "*self-worship.*" It might've been the most perfect expression of Western individualism I'd ever read.

Surprises were few when the Pew Research Centre reported the results of a survey of a thousand and thirty-three American Muslims from mid April to mid July, 2011. Forty-nine percent thought of themselves first as Muslim and only twenty-six percent first as American. That's the flaw with self-reporting; I was sure the reality was much more skewed towards Islam. The flaw recurred when only forty-six percent of American Christians thought of themselves first as Christians and the same proportion first as Americans. There will hardly be patriotic others, when there are so few patriotic us.

Asked my eldest son at the time, as fifteen-year-old boys should challenge their fathers, "What's wrong with that?"

For people believing in neither God nor Country, there's no conflict, as there isn't for people believing in one but not the other. Any religiously pluralistic country sets up a conflict between allegiances to religion and country. Muslims expect Muslim countries to honour Allah. Jews of faith expect Israel to honour Jehovah, although might argue what Jehovah demands. Nobody expects Western countries to honour God, but we used to expect it. We expected our churches to defend our countries, as other races' churches defend their people and countries. God and Country were the same loyalties. By not having both, the West ends up with neither.

Having lost interest in our peoples, we're preoccupied with our private little faiths. We pursue our perceived personal salvation, dwelling upon our inward senses of God without reference to religion. We do what we want to do; certain it's what God wants us to do, because we want steadfastly to do it. We settle upon our single-person beliefs with no regard for their effects upon others. Our compatriots do the same.

Headed to heaven without regard for the faith left on earth or the world after our far-coming deaths, our interests are in our afterlives, not anyone else's. We're self-contained Christians, not trying to retain or restore Christian countries. Religion has no link with our nation or society, because we have no nations or societies with which religion can link. For the sake of our small visions of ourselves, we walk away, while our compatriots can all go to hell.

2. COLLECTIVE GUILT

The most remarkable feature of people in places of worship isn't how different we are from people outside, but how similar. Western peoples of faith, whether in the Americas, Australasia, or Europe, are much like those without. We always were. We changed together.

Race more than religion defines people, however much we of European heritage now insist otherwise. Missionary wealth might have led the Tutsi (formerly called the Watusi) and most Hutus to call themselves Christian, but they were more tribal African than Christian during the Hutu genocides of Tutsi in Burundi in 1993 and Rwanda in 1994.

Christian white people are white more than Christian. Christian Chinese are Chinese more than Christian.

When Si Di interviewed Dave before our family's Uniting church the third Sunday in June 2013, Si Di asked Dave about the demographics of the two high schools at which Dave taught Scripture. Dave, being an Australian, said he didn't understand the question, but spoke of people being affluent by world standards. He answered about money. Si Di, being Chinese, explained that his question referred to multiculturalism. He asked about race.

Western churches are Western more than churches. Prepared for her by the youth pastor, the prayer my second daughter recited that Sunday began not with God but refugees.

We used to be Christian for being European. Being Western still determines our religion.

Our churches no longer lead the West, but follow. We don't interpret the Bible with open eyes and preach God's Word to the world. Instead, we accept whatever being Western implies. Without Biblical definition, we're free to redefine Christianity as we wish: less in God's image and more in ours. We've come to presume Christian obligations that aren't in the Bible, but are our postmodern impression of what goodness should be. We interpret the Bible accordingly, affirming what we want it to mean.

We call our resulting religion Christian, because we are Western. Biblical truth is something else altogether. We preach the West's word to God.

"They worship me in vain," said Christ, at chapter 15, verse 9 of the Gospel of Matthew, "their teachings are merely human rules." He could have been speaking of Western churches early in the twenty-first century.

There is no Biblical multiculturalism, individualism, or diversity. That is Western, and only recently. "Do not associate with these nations that remain among you," Joshua commanded the Israelites at Chapter 23, verse 7 of the Book of Joshua.

Christ did not eat with sinners to endorse their sins but to turn them from their sin. We can befriend people in sinful lifestyles without condoning their sins, but want them to heal from the pains that led them to those lifestyles and turn away from sin.

Verses 12 and 13 of chapter 5 in Paul's First Epistle to the Corinthians leave judging people outside the Church to God, but compel us to judge fellow churchgoers. "*Expel the wicked person from among you.*"

There is no Biblical command for inclusion or tolerance. They are Western commands, but only for us.

My childhood neighbour Bruce spoke of God choosing Christians as much as Christians choosing God. I thought then that was nonsense, but he was right. God chooses peoples and individuals. Peoples and individuals choose God.

The Bible speaks of believers and of God fearers. Nations, races, and other peoples encompass the faithful and the faithless.

The census in the Book of Numbers organised the nation of Israel into tribes and clans. Race, religion, and family are matters of blood. Being raised by Egyptians didn't make Moses less of an Israelite. It was religion by birth, by race.

God chose Europeans to spread His word. Chapter 13, verses 46 and 47 of the Book of Acts refer to God making the Apostle Paul and disciple Barnabas lights for the Gentiles, so as to bring salvation to the ends of the earth. (He may well have chosen other races too, if the Ethiopian eunuch that Philip baptised in chapter 8 of the Book of Acts is anything to go by.)

The robber (whose race we don't know) who repented from his cross beside Christ's Cross was the last Christian before the Crucifixion. The first Christians afterwards were Roman. "This

Man truly was the Son of God," said a centurion after seeing Christ's death, according to chapter 15, verse 39 of the Gospel of Mark. Several Roman centurions said the same after seeing Christ's death, feeling the earthquake, and with everything else they knew, according to chapter 27, verse 54 of the Gospel of Matthew.

Saint Peter and others brought the chance to be Christian to Rome, which brought the chance to the rest of Europe. When our European ancestors pursued the truth and believed in facts, they adopted Christianity because they knew it was true. Europeans took the chance to be Christian to the world. Most of the world didn't take it.

Races, for the most part, chose their religions. Those that freely adopted them (or bits and features of them) did so because those religions gelled with their natures or aspirations. We were peoples united not only by God, if not always by religious denominations. Races can also change their minds.

Since the Second World War, we've ceased thinking peoples chose God or that God chose peoples. There are no God's chosen people, least of all us. We aren't chosen by anyone. Nor are we people who'd once chosen God. We aren't a people at all but a motley array of individuals, except in matters of guilt. There, our aversion to race drops away.

Biblical guilt and innocence aren't just for individuals but for whole families and races, with the opportunities and responsibilities that entails. Goodness and favour spare not just the innocents but their families too, while whole peoples are punished and rewarded. The Book of Jeremiah, chapter 21 describes God punishing His people by bringing the king of Babylon to make them an everlasting ruin, but then punishing all Babylonians making them desolate forever. God's justice can be racial without diminishing His love.

In our postmodern, relativist frame of mind, facts are normally no more important to Western Christianity than to anything else we believe, but Mel Gibson's determination to be historically accurate in describing Jesus' Crucifixion in his 2004 film *The Passion of the Christ* was allegedly anti-Semitic. If the film was anti-Semitic, then so is the Bible. "I am innocent of this Man's blood," Pontius Pilate told the Jews. "It is your responsibility."

Trying to avert accusations of anti-Semitism, Gibson removed from his film's subtitles the Jews' response, according to chapter

27, verse 25 of the Gospel of Matthew. "His blood is on us and on our children!"

The passage was cited for centuries to say the Jews killed Christ: a collective, racial guilt brought upon all Jews by the actions of Jews described in the Bible. The Jewish Holocaust in 1945 ended our sense of Jewish racial guilt, although Nazi German dictator Adolf Hitler wouldn't have cared who killed Christ. In 1965, a Vatican II document, *Nostra Aetate*, declared that we couldn't attribute Jesus' death to all Jews.

I heard more mention of Christians blaming Jews for Christ's death during the 2007 British television programme *The Hidden Story of Jesus* than I'd heard through the rest of my life. Anti-Semitism still matters to the West, as Christianity no longer does.

The programme was broadcast in the Australian Broadcasting Corporation series *Compass*, which used to be about Christianity but had become about religion and how stupid Christians can be. Host Robert Beckford was black and so immediately attractive to white people as a spokesman for Christianity. He paid great deference to everything non-Christians said, while prefacing everything he said of Christianity with words like: "As a Christian, I was taught..." He would then realise what he'd been taught was wrong.

The people who taught him those supposed untruths might've been his parents, as they too had been duped, or his schoolteachers in England; we'd duped so many Africans. Beckford repeatedly insisted that our Christian accusation that Jews killed Christ was a lie, without consideration of it being sincere belief based upon Scripture. Yet, the programme included present-day Jews threatening to do to Jews adopting Christianity what they said their people did to Jesus two thousand years earlier. Beckford recognised they spoke as a people who'd killed Christ, after all.

The end of Jewish collective guilt ushered in Christian Europe's collective guilt. The Jews and we blame the Holocaust upon our past anti-Semitism.

Only eighteen, mostly elderly, parishioners attended the Epiphany service at our parish Anglican church early in 2014. After mentioning the Jewish authorities' complicity in the Massacre of the Innocents by the brutal part-Arab Jewish King Herod trying to kill baby Jesus, old Father John's sermon went onto criticise not Jews, Arabs, or racial mixing but anti-Semitism and the Church's past role in it. He claimed it led to the Holocaust.

"I have come to stand in silence before the monument erected to honour the millions of Jews killed in the horrific tragedy of the *Shoah*," said Pope Benedict XVI the second Monday in May 2009, standing at the Holocaust Memorial's darkened Hall of Remembrance in Jerusalem. "They lost their lives, but they will never lose their names. These are indelibly etched in the hearts of their loved ones, their surviving fellow prisoners, and all those determined never to allow such an atrocity to disgrace mankind again."

The Holy Father rekindled the eternal flame in the chamber, where the names of twenty-two of the most infamous Nazi murder sites were engraved in a mosaic floor. He laid a wreath over a stone crypt containing the ashes of Holocaust victims, signed the guest book, and sang '*Hatikva*'. Jews still weren't satisfied.

Rabbi Yisrael Meir Lau, the chairman of the Yad Vashem Council and a Holocaust survivor, was disappointed not to hear an apology. "If not an apology," he added, "then an expression of remorse."

Not merely must Christians ensure the Jews not suffer that atrocity again. We must feel the pain.

"We're talking about the Pope," said Knesset speaker Reuven Rivlin during an interview on Israel Radio, "who is also a representative of the Holy See, which has a lot to ask forgiveness from our people for." Sixty-four years after Christian and Soviet soldiers ended the Second World War and Holocaust, Jews still held the Roman Catholic Church accountable. "And he is also a German, whose country and people have asked forgiveness." He spoke as if Jews hadn't granted it. "There is one thing which is forbidden to forget, and we must not allow ourselves to forget it, not even in the act of giving up on it in one way or another due to protocol. The Holocaust is not protocol."

Jews feel forbidden to forget the Holocaust. So do we.

"I came to the memorial," said Rivlin, "not only to hear historical descriptions or about the established fact of the Holocaust. I came as a Jew, hoping to hear an apology and a request for forgiveness from those who caused our tragedy, and among them, the Germans and the Church, but to my sadness, I did not hear any such thing."

While we dwell upon our past attitudes to Jews, we ignore Jewish attitudes to us. To many Jews, we have traditionally been and remain *goyim*, or simply *goy*: amoral non-Jews, who Jews cannot trust. If *goy* is not necessarily derogatory in other contexts, then *sheigetz, shiksa,* and *shvartza* are, even if Jews do not use those Ashkenazic words in our presence.

"I was told never to read the New Testament because it was a Gentile handbook on how to persecute Jews," said American Jew Mottel Baleston in 2015, "but curiosity got the best of me." He became a Christian.

As only a person without religious conviction or confidence in his culture would, my second son's year-six teacher had adopted Judaism to marry a Jewess. "Oh, my god!" he often remarked, in spite of my son's Christian friend Ben telling him he found it offensive. Jews don't refer to god by name.

I used to be intrigued that Jews, like Woody Allen in his films, should complain "Jesus," until the evening service at our family's Uniting church mentioning the Ten Commandments. My mind a wandering, I realised the Torah commands Jews not to use the Lord God's name in vain. When Jews complain "Jesus," they're declaring Jesus not to be God. Western people complaining "Jesus" do the same.

"I'm Jewish," declared Mark Alan Siegel, the Palm Beach County chairman for the Democratic Party, in 2012. "I'm not a fan of any other religion than Judaism. The worst possible allies for the Jewish state are the fundamentalist Christians who want Jews to die and convert, so they can bring on the second coming of their Lord." At least Siegel was a man of conviction.

A significant number of Jews remain hostile to Christianity, as they're not to other religions. My Jewish friend Harry was an atheist, who wrote in the Facebook website the middle Wednesday of December 2014 of his *"personal belief...that religion is akin to voodoo."* He did so while defending Muslims after the Lindt Café siege two days earlier, in which two hostages died.

Harry offered no such defence to Christians. A week later, on Christmas Eve, he shared a picture bracketing Christianity with Nazism.

Much has been written about the relationship between the Holy See and Nazi Germany, even if little of it is ever read. Our simplistic summary of history is that the Church in Rome, like the rest of democratic Europe, feared the Soviet Union and worldwide revolution preached by atheistic communism more than we feared fascism. We appeased fascist regimes in Germany, Italy, Spain, and Portugal. "Blessed are the peacemakers," said Jesus.

In fact, Roman Catholic and Protestant churches opposed the rise of Nazism until, trying to survive under pressure from the Nazi regime, they compromised in a Concordat. The Nazis diluted clerical influence on religious instruction in public schools. They curbed the activities of religious schools, while influencing their curricula. Nazis supplanted Christian worship with secular celebrations adopting symbols of religious ritual (much as the West now does with multiculturalism), but glorified the Nazi Party and Hitler.

In 1937, Pope Pius XI issued the encyclical *Mit brennender Sorge* (With Burning Concern), which criticised Nazi philosophy. The Nazis responded with a wave of prosecutions of clergy. Churches spoke up on behalf of Jews who'd converted to Christianity and those married to parishioners, saving some lives, but lacked the cacophony of protest before 1939 we've come to demand with hindsight. Like the rest of Europe, including most Germans, the Church never imagined the Holocaust.

Jews weren't the only subjects of persecution at the time. Freemasonry had counted America's first president George Washington among its members and would care for my future father-in-law and his young siblings after their father died, but fascist Italy outlawed freemasonry in 1925. "Masonry must be destroyed, and masons should have no right to citizenship in Italy," said dictator Benito Mussolini. "To reach this end all means are good, from the club to the gun, from the breaking of windows to the purifying fire."

Yet, Mussolini couldn't comprehend Hitler's anti-Semitism: Jews owned shops. Only under pressure from Hitler did Italy pass anti-Semitic laws in 1938. When my father argued the foolishness of anti-Semitism, he cited Mussolini.

It's easy for Jews to treat Christians as being wrong: dismissing the New Testament, keeping the Old, and awaiting the Jew who'll be the messiah. I've not resolved what should be our approach to the Jews, if they were among God's people of the Old Testament who so rejected His Son in the New, but who suffered through the Holocaust.

We feel responsible for not saving them, but don't know what more we could have done. The fear of communism that seemed so pressing throughout the 1920s and '30s doesn't wash with us snug in the future.

Our racial and religious culpabilities remain intertwined, however much people's faiths falter. Christian faith endures among Copts, Filipinos, and other races nobody blames for the Holocaust. Neither Jews nor we hold the Caucasus countries of Armenia and Georgia culpable. Armenians know they're not participants but victims in matters of genocide.

However European peoples identify ourselves in other contexts, when it comes to our inherited guilt, we're not Jews, gypsies, or other foreigners or immigrants. The only people we're not are victims.

We confine Christian culpability, the culpability of Christendom, to the West. We weren't there, never killed anyone, but feel complicit in Christian Europe's crimes. No longer individuals when guilt consumes us, we're collectively culpable. Our individualism fails to absolve us, but we're trying hard to prevent repetition. Christian guilt is Western guilt. We're still Christendom after all.

It's collective religion like other races enjoy. All we lack is self-affection.

3. FEELING UNFORGIVEN

Religious inclusion lacks religious conviction. American Indians who reputedly tend to their ancient gods each morning and the European God each afternoon are trying to ensure they don't miss out either way.

Western multiculturalism doesn't just depend upon us trusting other religions. It depends upon us not trusting ours. We have let Christianity become offensive.

Nazi persecution began with requirements that Jews wear the Star of David, so the West became loath to make religion (any more than race) part of a person's identity. Religion wasn't a definition we applied to ourselves or anyone else, not anymore. Religion became private. Our lives became private. We each keep to ourselves.

We ceased foisting religion upon a person at birth, deciding that babies have no religion, nor idiots unable to think. Baptisms are our being born again into God, but few of our friends among the faithful still submit their babies for baptism. Most consider it pointless, that their children decide for themselves when they're old enough whether to be baptised.

I speak of what we do because it's what Western people do, even if my family and I don't. My wife and I offered our children for baptism soon after they were born, because we're not merely Christian individuals. We're a Christian family: Christian nuclear family, at any rate. I know how strange that makes us among European peoples. It used to be normal.

They'll be with us in heaven because the belief in Christ that brings them salvation remains a covenant with God unaffected if their faiths sadly wane. We enjoy eternal lives if, for at least one moment from the first to the last of our lives, we truly believe Jesus is the Son of God.

We were Christians by birth, before becoming Christians of faith. We can't change the circumstances of our birth.

Calling ourselves Christian mightn't bring us all into the bosom of God, but it's the belonging of being part of a people. Addressing St Ives Baptist Church about his journey to faith, retired newsreader Roger Climpson said his Christian childhood taught him the questions to ask when he was ready to ask. Most poignant of all was Climpson facing a medical crisis with the risk he would die by praying to God to save his life, if it be His will. When most of us would pray for life without caveat because it's our will, Climpson felt more humility and deference to God than many Christians of faith feel.

We might experience Christian schooling or other inductions into European or colonial European societies or feel Christian purely for our race. Let's face it: a person feeling part of a Christian people is far more likely to take up and keep Christian faith than a person who doesn't. With knowledge of our religion and God, however dormant, people can find belief in moments of old age, emptiness, or foreboding. They might learn love, joy, and belonging, comprehending a little of eternity to comfort them.

There's no more important idea in the world than the existence of God and that Christ is His Son: the God who so loved the world that He gave His Son to live among us and die in just punishment for our sins, before raising Him from the dead to reign with Him. There's no decision we make more important than our decisions about Them, or lack of decision, every day we're alive. Such decisions are more convincing for coming from our senses of being the people we are, than being our beliefs left alone. They're our mortality and immortality while we walk the earth, but mortality doesn't become immortality until our bodies die.

Our futures after we die depend upon us being Christian. Our futures until then depend upon us being a people: a Christian people, ideally.

Brother Ned Gerber told a five thirty service at our parish Anglican church that his parents and their generation thought Adolf Hitler was the anti-Christ. Ned didn't say whether that was during World War II or upon revelation of the Holocaust. Yet, hard as it is to imagine, if ever there were a moment in Hitler's tortured childhood before a tyrannical earthly father in which he truly believed Christ was the Son of God and chose for that one moment good over bad, then the implications are staggering. For such belief, if ever Hitler held it, he enjoys eternal life, in spite of his later actions: his sins washed away on the Cross with the rest of ours. Sin, life, and God are like that.

"*Therefore, there is now no condemnation for those who are in Christ Jesus,*" wrote the Apostle Paul at the start of chapter 8 of his Epistle to the Romans. We seem to have forgotten it. We are the Romans.

God forgives us our sins when we repent. We don't, not since the Second World War. We're consumed by all imaginable guilt for what we've done and think we've done in the past (before, during, and since the Holocaust), finding brief peace of mind or good conscience in our suffering and penance. We beg for the forgiveness of Jews for the Holocaust, but we need to forgive ourselves. We sinful selves can't have done more to repent, but it's still not enough.

In our determination to embrace Jews after the Holocaust, we brought Judaism into Christianity becoming Judeo–Christianity, so far as Christianity is concerned. (Judaism remains Judaism.) Ours is Old Testament guilt, Jewish guilt, without the redemption the Crucifixion offered. Our redefined Christianity leaves us with full buckets of guilt upon which we dwell endlessly, as if Christ didn't die to bleed guilt away. He just died.

When Archbishop Peter Jensen launched his Connect 09 community outreach on the second Sunday of February 2009, he spoke of the sinful city in which we lived headed for destruction. He might've been right, but in my chair in our parish Anglican church hall watching the broadcast, I cringed. Never did Christ's blood, hope, and salvation seem so far away.

Absent from our mouths is the joy we should celebrate for being alive and the good deeds we've done: the goodness within us described in the New Testament. "*For we are God's workmanship,*" enthused Paul at chapter 2, verse 10 of his Epistle to the Ephesians, "*created in Christ Jesus to do good works, which God prepared in advance for us to do.*"

There's no command from God to perform good works but the sense they're innate, at least to Paul and the Ephesians. "*For it is by grace you have been saved,*" he wrote in the preceding verses 8 and 9, "*through faith – and this not from yourselves, it is the gift of God – not by works, so that no one can boast.*"

Pride is a sin. We of the West think any sense of feeling good about ourselves is similarly sinful.

Most profoundly of all, Christianity alone among the major religions on earth made the death and resurrection of our Saviour stand centre stage in our faith. His death for the sins of the world brought redemption and purity again. It's a dramatic conflict between human failing and new-found perfection.

We've maintained the idea, although sins are now ours alone. God doesn't forgive sinners who never repent, but we think we're better than God. We forgive people for wrongs they've done against us without them repenting. We'd forgive them for wrongs against our race, if we ever imagined them wronging our race. Since the Holocaust, any thought of wrongs against our race became racist.

God loves us. We don't. Being Christian that used to bring us pleasure brings pain. Nailing ourselves to angst and principle, our last claim we're races and nations is how awful we are. Consumed by our sinfulness, we're the Church of Christendom's Self-Loathing.

Christ's ministry was radical during His time on earth, but that doesn't mean we should be radical. We should be Christ-like, which in particular contexts in our times and places might or might not be radical.

Robert Jensen, a journalism professor at the University of Texas in Austin (and, apparently, no relation to Peter Jensen), called himself a Christian radical. It was a strictly postmodern, multicultural Christianity and radicalism. In 2012, he wanted the "self-indulgent family feasting" of Thanksgiving, a "white supremacist holiday," replaced with "a National Day of Atonement accompanied by a self-reflective collective fasting." That, he thought, would be "moral progress," because of our "original sin – the genocide of indigenous people."

No other race of religion is so cruel to itself. If the Jews aren't still punishing us for the Holocaust, then we're punishing our pernicious selves.

What with the problems people say our religion has caused, English theologian Theo Hobson called himself post-Anglican. Not just expecting the Church of England's demise, he looked forward to it.

Trying to be innocent of Christendom's crime, Hobson saw liberal guilt as a political expression of having a conscience. (Other races presumably have either no consciences or nothing for which to feel guilty.) Our shame and guilt have become virtues.

There's no end of things for which Hobson felt we should feel guilt, including the weather. "*Similarly*," he wrote in 2010, "*there is no excuse for failing to feel liberal guilt about race and class. The fact is that it is excessively hard for the vast majority of people from ethnic minorities, and from economically disadvantaged backgrounds, to attain the cushy lifestyle that one was born into and takes for granted.*"

Yet, if there'd been no divisions by class then the ruling classes would never have admitted immigrants from other races, creating ethnic minorities. We're no less divided by class in our churches than outside. Ours is guilt for the lifestyle our forefathers and mothers earned and bequeathed us, which we've not yet given away.

It gets worse. Reverend Peter Adam, principal of Ridley College, an Anglican theological college in Victoria, epitomised our unending self-hatred when giving the New South Wales Baptist Union's annual lecture at Morling College, Macquarie Park in August 2009. He accused Australians of genocide against Aborigines merely for settling the country two hundred and twenty-one years earlier. "No recompense could ever be satisfactory, because what was done was so vile, so immense, so universal, so pervasive, so destructive, so devastating, and so irreparable." We hold our people and past in deep contempt.

Adam had no sense of Europeans building Australia, only stealing it. "The prosperity of our churches has come from the proceeds of crime. Our houses, our churches, our colleges, our shops, our sport grounds, our parks, our courts, our parliaments, our prisons, our hospitals, our roads, our reservoirs are stolen property."

Sounding shrill, he wasn't imagining Aborigines building those things without us; they're too wonderful to have created monstrosities. Adam saw no value in the country we'd built, only harm.

He claimed Christian teaching required restitution to the Aboriginal people (presumably removing the houses, churches, and colleges we'd built, including his own) or us to pay compensation, but there is no such Christian teaching. "It would in fact be possible, even if very difficult and complicated, for Europeans and others to leave Australia," said Adam. "I am not sure where we would go, but that would be our problem." (I couldn't imagine him wanting immigrants to leave Europe.)

Too accommodating of Nazi Germany through her early years,

too much defending our races and averting war through the 1930s instead of saving Jews, we keep trying to atone. Striving to clean ourselves, we stay dirty.

Adam was no less estranged from people than from God. The Ridley College website said of him, "*He enjoys reading history and fiction, playing the piano, and being walked by his dog George.*"

The Cross of Christ's death burns in our souls. Only the West conceives we should hand up our countries, cultures, and races, our churches and parishioners, to aid other races. We can't conceive of anything else.

In psychological terms, we're immersed in a massive saviour complex: sacrificing ourselves to save not our people but everyone else. Other races can be as wretched, corrupt, and pathetic as any sin can be, committing monstrous evil against us, but we're too arrogant to think God or anyone but us can save them. If we don't love ourselves and don't think God loves us, others have no reason to like us.

We never seem more Christ-like than in our capacity for self-sacrifice, but we've redefined what sacrifice should be. Christ sacrificed His life for us. We're not sure why we're dying, we saviours of the world, although we know something's good about it. His action was incredibly heroic, in spite of His Resurrection. Mortal men and women dishonourably giving up their lives aren't heroic. Our racial penitence doesn't change other peoples' histories. We self-serving individuals would rather sacrifice each other, but collectively as sacrificial Christendom, we're sacrificing us all.

Christ having given up His life for us means we don't need to give up our lives so easily, as we now are. We're dying unloved, most notably by ourselves. We keep trying to save the mortal world but it stays mortal, at our mortal and immortal cost. To serve God saving the world, sensing Him at our shoulders, we need not to die but endure.

4. DISCRIMINATION

Adam and Eve might have been metaphorical. They might have been the first of our race, or theirs. All people might not be related. Who were the people Cain feared harming him after he murdered his brother Abel, mentioned at the Book of Genesis, chapter 4, verse 13? From where did Cain's wife come?

The people that survived the Great Flood in Noah's Ark lived and travelled eastward together, speaking a single language, until God fractured them into a multitude of languages at the Tower of Babel, described at Genesis, chapter 11. In a condemnation of multiculturalism and globalism, God used language to affirm that people are of different tribes. He scattered them into separate nations around the earth.

So we all remained, until after the Second World War. Dispensing with religious loyalties after the Holocaust, Western churches and schools were at the forefront of turning our racial loyalties upside down. Race and religion are much too intertwined, especially for Jews, for our opposition to religious discrimination not to be opposition to racial discrimination. There's no turning the other cheek to white people's racism.

Late in the 1960s and early '70s, Lindsay Tanner attended Gippsland Grammar School. He would go onto become one of the so-called "gang of four" running the show that was the Australian government in 2008, and for a while there appeared most likely to become the next prime minister. Calling himself an agnostic Anglican, the first time I came across such a term, he often spoke of his boyhood boarding at the school. "I was subject to brutality bordering on abuse," he said in May 2008, "not sexual abuse, no, but physical."

In his Redmond Barry Lecture later that year, Tanner described, as he often described, how at least one Aboriginal boy escaped that brutality. "In those days, the White Australia policy was still in place, indigenous Australians were treated with contempt, and other peoples were portrayed through ridiculous stereotypes. Yet the Anglican Church worked hard to instil a more enlightened view into me and my fellow boarders." Tanner's was our interpretation post Holocaust of what constitutes enlightenment.

"This went beyond complacent sermonising and glib pieties. Our boarding house of about sixty boys included Aboriginal, Thai, and Indian kids. Whenever race was an issue, the message from those in authority was clear and unequivocal.

"When I was thirteen, an indigenous classmate who occupied the bed next to mine got involved in a confrontation with another kid in our dormitory. Harmless horseplay turned nasty when he accidentally trod on this boy's foot and hurt him. He was promptly hit with a volley of racist abuse, and being a good boxer, he responded with his fists. Within minutes, both boys were in the housemaster's office. We were routinely caned for such trivialities as talking after lights out and dirty phys. ed. gear, so I expected my indigenous mate would be caned.

"Much to my surprise, he wasn't. The message was clear. The sticks and stones rule didn't apply to racial abuse. His physical assault was overlooked, because of the racist provocation. In 1960s rural Australia, this was pretty unusual. Yet the school's position reflected deeply entrenched values of decency and openness, a willingness to allow people to succeed or fail on their merits, not the colour of their skin." (That supposed decency didn't save Tanner from suffering brutality.) "These values made it possible for us to make the transition from the world of the White Australia policy to modern multicultural Australia."

Tanner quoted a Victorian Equal Opportunity and Human Rights Commission report, saying "While much of the blatant racism and name-calling is a thing of the past, the discrimination people face today is more subtle, entrenched and much more difficult to identify and deal with." (No doubt, Tanner would've accepted that as good cause for other races to bash us senseless.)

Tanner's life was defined by his efforts to advance other races, often at the expense of his own: protesting against South Africa's apartheid regime and in favour of East Timor independence; aiding African immigrants to Australia with a passion he never offered his compatriots. He did it all without faith in God, but presumably the approval of Gippsland Grammar School.

Western Christians dwell upon men and women being made in the image of God (whatever that means) in chapter 1, verses 26 and 27 and chapter 9, verse 6 of the Book of Genesis as a reason to embrace every person on earth. Doing so disregards everything else in the Bible.

The Bible doesn't just condone racial and religious discrimination. It makes it. Chapter 21, verses 2 to 11 of the Book of Exodus, chapter 15, verses 12 to 18 of the Book of Deuteronomy, and chapter 34, verse 14 of the Book of Jeremiah mandate masters giving slaves and their families freedom after seven years in certain circumstances, but only if the slaves are Hebrew.

(Much is now made of the Bible condoning slavery as a reason to disregard the Bible, but the Bible only condones slavery to repay debts, much like indentured servitude, and in war. The Apostle Paul interpreted slavery much as we might interpret employment; I've seen jobs like that. In chapter 6 of his Epistle to the Ephesians, Paul called upon slaves to obey their masters, but masters to treat their slaves the same way. In the first two verses of chapter 6 of his First Epistle to Timothy, he acknowledged the yoke of slavery, but expected Christian masters to commit to their slaves' welfare. The Bible condemns trading in slaves.)

Biblical discrimination is often religious. Chapter 2, verse 11 of the Book of Malachi condemns those who have *"desecrated the sanctuary the Lord loves by marrying women who worship a foreign god."* Predicting that God would kill those men, Malachi insisted they divorce (although at verse 16, he generally condemns divorce).

Some Biblical discrimination mixes race and religion, because different races have different religions. The first four verses of Chapter 7 of the Book of Deuteronomy prohibit Israelites from marrying people of seven nations mightier than they are. They prohibit Israelites from taking those women for their sons or giving their daughters to those men because the resulting children will turn away from them, worshipping other gods.

Much Biblical discrimination is explicitly racial, especially around marriage. Allowing interracial marriage because God created every race would be like allowing bestiality because God created animals too.

Chapter 10, verses 10 and 11 of the Book of Leviticus describe the son of an interracial marriage as a blasphemer. At verse 16, he is put to death.

Interracial marriage is blasphemy. Reconciliation with God

requires people to send away their foreign wives and mixed-race children.

Deuteronomy, chapter 23, prohibits Israelites from marrying some races but allows them to marry Edomites (a related race, almost the same) and Egyptians, making the third generation Israelite. Some Egyptians joined Moses in the Exodus.

Whatever races might be closely enough related to fall within the exemptions to Biblical prohibitions on miscegenation, if any do, are of the nature we might call ethnic groups. Whether fellow Europeans are similarly related races for Europeans to marry them is not clear. Scots and Irish might not be closely enough related.

At Chapter 23, verses 12 and 13 of the Book of Joshua, Joshua warns the Israelites that "if you turn away and ally yourselves with the survivors of these nations that remain among you and if you intermarry with them and associate with them, then you may be sure that … they will become snares and traps for you, whips on your backs and thorns in your eyes, until you perish from this good land, which the Lord your God has given you."

"We have been unfaithful to our God by marrying foreign women from the peoples around us," Shekaniah, son of Jehiel, told Ezra at chapter 10, verses 2 and 3 of the Book of Ezra, "but in spite of this, there is still hope for Israel. Now let us make a covenant before our God to send away all these women and their children, in accordance with the counsel of my lord and of those who fear the commands of our God. Let it be done according to the Law."

Ezra, chapter 9, condemns marriages *"that mingle the holy race."* Ours was the race that shared Christianity with the world. We might be the holy race, even if we've lost track of it.

Becoming Abraham's seed means Europeans were always heirs to the promise. Having been his heirs, we can never cease.

Chapter 13, verse 27 of the Book of Nehemiah condemns those *"being unfaithful to our God by marrying foreign women?"* Ezra and Nehemiah also insisted Jews divorce their spouses who weren't Jewish, with Nehemiah saying at verse 30: *"I purified the priests and the Levites of everything foreign."* Chapter 44, verse 22 of the Book of Ezekiel requires priests to marry only Israelite virgins or other priests' widows.

Whatever God was, He still is. He didn't change when Jesus was born. Only our understanding of Him did.

"I was sent only to the lost sheep of Israel," Jesus tells the woman at chapter 15, verse 24 of the Gospel of Matthew. She calling Him Lord led to Jesus healing her daughter because she demonstrated she was among the people to whom Jesus was sent.

Jesus might have referred to the Israelites being lost sheep, for whom He would first fulfil Old Testament prophecy for the Israelites before sharing His message with the rest of the world. That would not explain why He promptly healed the woman's daughter when she called Him Lord, when He had not yet finished fulfilling Old Testament prophecy.

Alternatively, Jesus might have meant Israel to encompass anyone who recognised Him as Lord. The Israelites were aware, or ought to have been aware, that He was sent for them. Greeks and other Europeans, and perhaps more races, turning to Christ would have been hitherto unknown tribes of Israelites: allegorical tribes of Israel, or the lost sheep of Israel.

The New Testament doesn't shy away from generalisations with racial connotations, although identifying the race along with the geography can be problematic. *"Even one of their own prophets has said,"* wrote Paul at chapter 1, verse 12 of his Epistle to Titus, a Greek in charge of the church in Crete, *"'Cretans are always liars, evil brutes, lazy gluttons.' This testimony is true."* If Paul was quoting the Greek philosopher Epimenedes in the seventh or sixth century before Christ, Paul would have referred to Epimenedes as one of *"your"* own prophets in his Epistle to Titus. A large proportion of Crete's residents were Jews.

In our postmodern parlance, Paul is a bigot. The Bible being divinely inspired, God is also a bigot.

The Bible and loving God remain racist and nationalistic without diminishing the opportunity Christ brought all people and races to follow Him. Some do. Others don't. We used to.

"There is neither Jew nor Gentile, neither slave nor free, nor is there male and female, for you are all one in Christ Jesus," wrote Paul at chapter 3, verses 28 and 29 of his Epistle to the Galatians. *"If you belong to Christ, then you are Abraham's seed, and heirs according to the promise."*

Christian slaves were no less Christian than Christian free people. Different roles for men and women did not make one Christian but not the other.

People who think Paul's words mean race isn't real must also think they mean gender isn't real. No more denying one than the other, Paul was simply telling the Galatians they could retain their Celtic and other European culture without needing to adopt Jewish ritual. Jews becoming Christians could keep their Jewish culture. European peoples becoming Christians could keep ours.

Biblical oneness is only between Christians. Race and gender remain, while we're equally Christian.

Judaism requires Jews to marry fellow Jews. Islam requires Muslims to marry fellow Muslims.

Islam doesn't recognise marriages with people of other religions. The West practically demands them. Suggesting marriages across religions are more likely to fail doesn't suit our multicultural vision, even when one party converts to the other's religion, but it remains intuitively true.

One couple presenting a happy, loving home told the District Court in 2010 their happiness was a lie. (Judge Stephen Norrish ordered their names be suppressed, to protect them and their families overseas from harm.) "*The sad reality of being caught between Eastern culture and Western values, they told a court,*" said the *Sydney Morning Herald* newspaper. (Western multiculturalism means other races have cultures, we have values.) "*The man, a professional in his home country, had converted to Islam in order for the couple's marriage to be legally recognised. But when they separated after moving to Australia, they maintained the outward appearance of a married couple to avoid physical harm, or even death, at the hands of Islamic extremists back home, they claimed. Under Islamic law, marriage between a Muslim woman and a non-Muslim man is not legally recognised and would be considered an adulterous relationship. Such a union is usually considered proper and legal if a religious conversion takes place.*"

An Islamic law expert (who the newspaper didn't name) saw the risk of violence from Muslims. The failure of marriages where a spouse converted to Islam or without family blessing "could have been perceived as proof that these sort of relationships don't work or it could be perceived as additional harm to the family name, reopening old wounds."

People of religious conviction rarely marry outside their religion, just as people valuing their cultures rarely marry people of other cultures; there's too much they can't share with their spouse. People identifying with their families don't divide their families by marrying people at odds with their family identity: their race and religion. There are no multicultural families. There are just multicultural households.

The only child of a Jewish father and Roman Catholic Hungarian mother, Warren's parents let him choose his religion; neither parent offered him conviction. He chose Judaism, stunning me with the effort he'd made in seeming to memorise an hour-long speech in Hebrew for the only bar mitzvah I've attended. (Many decades later, he admitted he had not memorised as much as appeared.) He might have longed for belonging, when Christian Europe was becoming unimportant. Jewish identity remained.

Julian was a religiously devout Jew, who'd embraced a notion of Western civilisation both Jewish and Christian so much that he married an Australian. Her Christian faith can't have been too important to her. She had agreed their children would be raised Jews.

Without Western Christianity offering reason to be Christian, the children of multicultural marriages are choosing their other parent's cultures, if their biology does not choose for them. Michael Zehaf-Bibeau's father was a Libyan businessman and mother was a Canadian who joined the Immigration and Refuge Board of Canada as a refugee protection officer. They divorced in 1999. His mother raised him in her Roman Catholicism but he converted to his father's Islam, before shooting dead Corporal Nathan Cirillo, a young father in Ottawa, and attacking the nearby Centre Block parliament building in 2014.

5. POSTMODERN CHRISTIANITY

Traditionally, Christ's Resurrection proved He was the Son of God, inspiring His Apostles to live and die for Him. Lord Darling, an English High Court judge who died in 1936, believed there was more than enough evidence to convince a jury of Jesus' Resurrection.

When presented with a quote by Darling at St Ives Baptist Church the second Sunday in August 2015, former Australian attorney general Bob Ellicott suggested the Resurrection wasn't a physical event. Ellicott said it was merely the realisation by others of Jesus' divinity.

That plainly was not what Darling meant. Ellicott didn't suggest what might have caused the Disciples' realisation of Christ's divinity, after they abandoned Him before His death. The Crucifixion gutted them.

Without Christ's immortality restored by the Resurrection, Western Christianity becomes much like Western atheism. Also believing Biblical text without believing Christ to be the Son of God, my atheist friend Don Wormald thought Son of God referred to any head of a sect at the time.

Only three American television series I've seen included regular characters identified as being Christian. Ned Flanders in *The Simpsons* was a joke. Father Tim Flotsky in *Soap* left the priesthood because a woman pursued him, married her, and left her. Major Burns in *M*A*S*H* was a patriotic American who prayed, but was also a snivelling, incompetent, materialistic adulterer. They all made Christians look bad. Burns also made patriotic Americans look bad.

The only good Christian character was the well-meaning but inconsequential Father Mulcahy, also in *M*A*S*H*. He was the sort of priest we liked, with the sort of Christianity we tolerated. He never preached. I don't recall him mentioning God at all, although he might once or twice have pointed his finger to the sky and smiled. If modernism is the West without faith in being

Western and postmodernism is the West without faith in anything, then ours is a postmodern Christianity, without faith in being Western or in God. Western Christianity became inoffensive.

We used to think our relative prosperity was reason to believe in ourselves, God, and countries. It's become another reason not to believe in them.

Bob Hawke was the son of a church minister, but called himself agnostic after attending the 1952 World Christian Youth Conference in Kottayam. Seeing the poverty in India didn't diminish his faith in Indians or Hinduism; that would be racist. It diminished his faith in God.

As prime minister, Hawke led the Labor Party to the 1987 federal election with a promise to ensure no Australian child lived in poverty. The only point of the promise was winning the election and so it succeeded. Three years later, there'd been no reduction in the numbers of poor children, but poverty in Australia didn't diminish Hawke's faith in himself. When the Brotherhood of St Laurence tried to hold him to account, Hawke was furious, accusing Anglican archbishop Peter Hollingworth of being party to an "untrue, unchristian bloody statement."

Western Christianity is no longer a theistic religion but, for many who don't damn it outright, a matter of kindness, particularly to them. To be Christian is to be amenable, agreeing with people whatever nonsense they express.

In 1989, Father Bob Maguire was awarded an Order of Australia for his services to the community. Twenty-two years later, seventy-seven years old and about to retire, he delivered his last Christmas message. "A bit old-fashioned," he said, erroneously, "but I think if you put somebody else first at Christmas, I think you're probably doing the most religious thing you could possibly do." (Worshipping God, or even attending Maguire's Roman Catholic church in South Melbourne, weren't so religious.) "A lot of people do remarkably generous and kind things, all day, every day, and they don't go near churches, you see what I mean? So I'm saying to do good is to do God."

There's not much we don't permit. The first Saturday in 2012, Maguire allowed a witch, Eilish De Avalon, to conduct a pagan hand-fasting ceremony after a wedding in St James Church, Brighton. Hand-fasting ceremonies could be performed for couples whatever their combinations of genders and for multiple partners.

They involved the parties' hands being tied together, making vows usually for a year and a day afterwards, and sometimes jumping over a broomstick. De Avalon ignored Maguire's wish that she tone back her script in a church.

Our goodness has become gullibility. "I was taken for a ride and blindsided," Maguire admitted. "Once in the saddle, she took over the place. It was like the Devil got a hold of me."

Maguire became the subject of the 2013 documentary *In Bob We Trust*. He'd supplanted God.

In Pope Francis' desire to reach out to those without Christian faith in 2013, he wrote an open letter to the founder of *La Repubblica* newspaper, Eugenio Scalfari, dispensing with Biblical teaching altogether. *"God's mercy has no limits if you go to him with a sincere and contrite heart. The issue for those who do not believe in God is to obey their conscience. Sin, even for those who have no faith, exists when people disobey their conscience."*

We presume so much goodness in people and that people are so much the same, but conscience formed in isolation is more individualism. Conscience formed among evil people is evil.

Christianity becomes a religion without God: Christendom without Christ, Christless Christianity, indistinguishable from other charity. We've changed the Biblical statement that God is love from one about God to one about love.

Nothing in the Bible suggests love alone makes somebody Christian. John the Evangelist wrote of God being love in his First Epistle, chapter 4, verse 16, amidst his advices on how Christians could distinguish people and teachings of God from those that are not of God. Satanists might believe Jesus Christ is the Son of God as Christians do, but we know they're not of God because they lack love. They're not coming from the Father or to Him as Christ intended. John may well have attributed all love ultimately to God, but God remains distinct from love.

In her eulogy for the late Reverend Keith Dowding in 2008, Melissa Parke told the Australian parliament of what she called Dowding's Christian socialism. Lauding his campaigns to allow interracial immigration and homosexuality, the reverend she described was neither Christian nor socialist. If God was part of his story, Parke felt no need to mention it.

Amidst our rights to pick and choose religion unfettered by matters of fact, many atheists and agnostics refuse to recognise

God because of His nature or commands with which they disagree, especially those related to race and sexuality. They're more Biblically sound than Christians who simply ignore or interpret away those commands. God becomes someone with whom we agree. It's our condition upon which we're willing to believe that He's real, in the most extraordinary arrogance human beings have ever displayed.

Australian tennis great Margaret Court's opposition to homosexual marriage in 2012 led to calls for her name to be removed from Melbourne Park centre court. In an interview, she referred to homosexuals who'd come to her church, "and you'll find that many, many of them have been abused." She was then asked if she believed such abuse led people to homosexuality. "Yes," she replied. "You look at a lot of them, that's happened." Court also complained about immigrants expecting Australians "to change our laws to embrace what they have, and I don't feel that's right."

Court was a Christian of faith, but ours is a postmodern church. Peter Rosengren, editor of the Roman Catholic Church newspaper *The Record*, said he'd "never heard of any scientific study" linking abuse and homosexuality. (We don't make those kinds of study anymore, without being certain we can construct the answers we want.) He said that "everyone has to be respected," which means we don't try to help them.

People feeling loved by God love themselves. They want to survive: to procreate. Theirs is not the superficial self-absorption of the narcissistic, or of the deeply hurting.

Presuming that people can never be victims of their own actions, Richard Holloway, previously the Primus of the Episcopal Church of Scotland, wanted the Church in 2001 to keep out of what he called "victimless crimes," by which he included homosexuality and drug use. He could've said the same about laws mandating use of seatbelts and controlling sales of tobacco; we used to like God being paternalistic. Holloway wanted the Church to be "open and inclusive and affirming."

We're not affirming Christianity but individualism: individuals thinking whatever they think and doing whatever they do, however destructive they're being. Treating self-harm as a victimless crime rejects every sense that harm to a person also harms that person's family, race, and the world at large. Believing "the Bible has to move with the times," Holloway effectively meant we should rewrite and continue rewriting the Bible to whatever we want the Bible to say.

Atheists agree. Journalist Sam de Brito said the Reverend Fred Nile's opposition to homosexual marriage in 2013 *"doesn't sound very Christian to me."*

Jesus didn't think so. At chapter 19, verse 5 of the Gospel of Matthew and chapter 10, verses 7 and 8 of the Gospel of Mark, Jesus repeated words from chapter 2, verse 24 of the Book of Genesis: *"That is why a man leaves his father and mother and is united to his wife, and they become one flesh."*

Christ recognised human nature. Everybody did, then.

Jesus said little about morality, because moral right and wrong were already well known to His audiences. At chapter 15, verse 19 of the Gospel of Matthew, Jesus listed among evil thoughts what the Greeks called *porneia*, or sexual immorality, along with murder, adultery, theft, lying, and slander. At chapter 7, verse 21 of the Gospel of Mark, that list also included coveting, wickedness, envy, pride, and foolishness. Jesus' audiences knew that sexual immorality included men lying with men.

Paul was more explicit. Chapter 1, verse 10 of Paul's First Epistle to Timothy explicitly condemns homosexuality. Morals would remain well known for another two thousand years, until the West lost sight of them.

Not satisfied with ignoring the repeated and explicit Biblical condemnation of homosexuality, the third edition of the New Oxford Annotated Bible published in 2000 (which referred to the Old Testament as the Hebrew Bible to accommodate Jews) expurgated homosexuality altogether from the sixth chapter of Paul's First Epistle to the Corinthians. *"Do not be deceived,"* wrote Paul in verses 9 and 10, except in the New Oxford Annotated Bible. *"Neither the sexually immoral, nor idolaters, nor adulterers, nor men who have sex with men, nor thieves, nor the greedy, nor drunkards, nor slanderers, nor swindlers, will inherit the kingdom of God."*

Hardly words the West likes, removing homosexuality was more important than removing those other immoralities. We choose items of Christianity, much as we choose items of haberdashery.

The Bible is no longer God's word. It is now our word.

That Paul mentioned homosexuality along with sexual immorality did not mean that sexual immorality did not already include homosexuality. Sexual immorality included adultery too. Wondering what led Paul to emphasise homosexuality is like wondering what led Jesus and Paul to emphasise adultery.

If God is love because He loves us, then God is science too. Everything the Bible teaches about sexuality, family, and race reflects our natures, with the explanation obvious: God created us. None of it is arbitrary. We understand Biblical teaching by study and reason.

We've ceased studying or paying attention to reason. Western Christians believe God makes some people homosexual, because the West believes some people are born homosexual. It's like saying God makes some people necrophiliacs, bank robbers, or chiropodists. People in church abrogate personal responsibility, much like people outside.

Our postmodern churches are more postmodern than churches. In the conflict between God and homosexuality, we're laying out the sheets.

Nativity scenes outside the Claremont United Methodist Church, California each Christmas focus not upon Jesus but upon political causes. A depiction of the fence along the Mexican border suggested America should have no national borders. So estranged are we from reverence for parenthood, a mother and baby in prison was less about babies than about gaols. "Christ's birth in a stable had a lot to do with poverty and being marginalised," said Pastor Sharon Rhodes-Wickett in 2011, less interested in what it had to do with God. "What this church has tried to do through these scenes is say, 'What would that look like today?'"

She answered the question not with Biblical scholarship, but Western individualism. Artist John Zachary had created a scene in which three couples stood under a Star of Bethlehem and sign that "*Christ is Born*," but the star and sign were incidental. Only one of the three couples was a man and woman. The others were two men and two women. The church had welcomed homosexuals since 1993.

Instead of society we have social justice, in which Reverend Nicole Fleming described her Uniting church congregation in Balmain, Sydney as being united. A week after her induction in July 2011, Ben Gilmour became minister of Paddington Uniting church. Both were homosexual.

Instead of the Bible, our postmodern churches often have

mission statements, typically less about Christianity than about inclusion. Church doors have always been open to people without Christian faith, perhaps wanting to learn something about it. Today, we welcome homicidal Satanists.

The Brentwood Christian Church, Missouri mission statement in August 2012 was a long list of people it welcomed, including people who *"believe in God some of the time or none of the time or all of the time."* Devout Christians were last in the list.

Reverend Phil Snider delivered a speech apparently against homosexual marriage before the Springfield City Council, at the end of which he said his words were all from speeches in the 1950s and '60s defending racial segregation. "The right of segregation is clearly established by the Holy Scriptures, both by precept and example."

In 2012, racial integration was an accepted truism in the West. Snider thought that implied homosexual marriage should be too. Had any preacher equated racial integration with homosexual marriage in the 1950s and '60s, he would have been laughed off the pulpit.

Hot on the heels of homosexuality came so-called transgenderism, although chapter 22, verse 5 of the Book of Deuteronomy could hardly be more explicit. *"A woman must not wear men's clothing, nor a man wear women's clothing, for the Lord your God detests anyone who does this."*

Postmodern Christianity follows the rest of the West into redefining man and woman away from human biology and nature so as to make a mockery of the passage. It is inconceivable that God would cease detesting a transvestite because he identifies as a woman.

Like much of history, our downward trajectory since the two world wars is more obvious with hindsight than it would have been to predict beforehand. Before then, our forebears feared we'd lose our Western mores to other races' sexual plays and decadence if we let them close. If we'd confined ourselves to African heterosexual promiscuity we took up through the 1960s and '70s, it might not have been so bad.

If churches aren't following God's natural laws, the faithful have little reason to remain. My in-laws believe Adamstown Uniting church lost many of its parishioners because the church appointed a lesbian minister.

Where inclusion (and asylum seekers) matter more than God and Christianity, morality is obsolete. My family left our family Uniting church in 2016 because most church elders were relaxed, if not enthusiastic, about the youth and young adult pastor entering into a lesbian relationship with a troubled young woman supposedly her responsibility.

(That troubled young woman's social media page had previously said she was interested in boys. The pastor had only spoken of relationships with males, although that had been long ago. She was well into her thirties and unmarried.)

The recently appointed family and children's pastor also resigned, leaving the Uniting church altogether. He and his wife were raising daughters.

Inclusion is selective. Reverend Laurel, perhaps with other elders, had ensured the elders' forum considered the pastor's lesbianism in the absence of the chairman of the congregation and of the church council. Unusually among Western church figures, Phill retained a moral code and Christian faith. With no need for expedition, Laurel expedited consideration of the issue while Phill was overseas.

If Reverend Laurel thought that Phill would come around to other elders' views, having with his wife Julie given so much to the church and its parishioners for so long, then she was wrong. Phill and Julie also left the church. Between them, they had attended the church and its predecessor for more than ninety years.

6. MULTICULTURAL CHRISTIANITY

In 2013, Pope Francis canonised the eight hundred and thirteen Italian martyrs of the city of Otranto in 1480. He omitted to mention they were executed by Turks for refusing to convert to Islam.

At his talk in our parish Anglican church hall the first Sunday night in September 2011, Bishop Michael condemned tribalism and individualism. I wondered what remained.

Only multiculturalism remains. Fusing Christianity with Judaism after the Holocaust, the West ultimately fused our faith with every other religion too. Without conviction in Christianity, we're more certain of cultural equality than a European God.

The tenets of multiculturalism fill the void of postmodern Christianity. All cultures are equal. *Ipso facto*, all religions are equal. Thus God is equally manifest through different religions. Rather than letting religion be a barrier to us creating a single world civilisation, Western Christianity becomes a facet of a single world religion, much like any other.

We overcome the problems of pluralism with a new religious homogeneity. By reducing Christianity to the same as all other religions, we demonstrate our inclusiveness. Nothing's more important to us, not even salvation.

Embracing other cultures, we seize upon any hint of commonality with ours and ignore glaring differences. Deeming all religions equal is an ideology. It depends upon a complete lack of theological scrutiny and other analysis.

"I am the way and the truth and the life," said Jesus, according to chapter 14, verse 6 of the Gospel of John. "No one comes to the Father except through Me."

Falling foul of Him doesn't deter us. Wrapping our arms around the world, we effectively rewrite Jesus' words. "You can come to God by whatever way you like: Me, you, Mohammed, Buddha, Mrs Fields' Cookies…"

Caring less about our faith than others, we've reduced religion as we've reduced race: to a universal sameness. Our belief in God includes believing everything else; anything else would be rude. We're much like the Baha'i (something of a non-religion anyway, multicultural to start with), without being Baha'i. Our multicultural Christianity is a Judeo–Christian fusion neither Jewish nor Christian.

Multiculturalism has supplanted Christianity for the West. Ideology has supplanted religion.

We premise it upon our confidence in other cultures. They don't need any notion of God.

Nothing in the Aboriginal Dreamtime stories or much else about Aboriginal life before Europeans came was akin to Christianity. Nevertheless, in 2009, the twelfth Assembly of the Uniting Church adopted a preamble to its constitution that, at paragraph 3, claimed *"Aboriginal law, custom, and ceremony"* was the *"Spirit"* revealing *"the Creator God"* to Aborigines. *"The same love and grace that was finally and fully revealed in Jesus Christ sustained the First Peoples and gave them particular insights into God's ways."* (It also imagined Aborigines having complex systems of *"trade and inter-relationships."*)

Citing a scene in the 1982 film *Gandhi*, Bishop Michael believed Mahatma Gandhi exemplified Jesus' response to violence. The bishop seemed uninterested that Gandhi was a Hindu Indian opposed to the bishop's forebears: the Christian British Army. (In all events, the bishop was an odd person to laud peaceful resistance. At his last diocese, he'd been subject to thirteen complaints by parishioners and clergy, including allegations of bullying.)

He and a few parishioners in the audience went onto wonder where God had been through the suffering of people with God in them doing God's will, but they weren't referring to Christians. They referred to the Libyan Revolution half a year long, which had just toppled Muammar Gaddafi. They spoke oblivious to Libyans being Muslim.

Now, I can understand people asking where God has gone when hurricanes strike, although anything less than a world where we all live to the same predictable age with the same health and abilities would be tedious. Our fragility amidst the potential for sudden tragedy brings meaning and dimension to life. When

Christians kill, it's reasonable to ask what's happening with Christianity among those Christians. When we're victims of other religions, we might feel abandoned by God. Christ did on the Cross. Jews did in the Holocaust.

I seemed to be the only person wondering how other races felt about our multicultural theism. Installing God in the minds of people not Christian is presumptuous, if not absurd. That's not to say God mightn't use people of other religions to further His plans, but I imagined Libyans laughing to learn Western churches imagined our God in their Muslim lives. If they weren't laughing, they might've been offended.

Muslims don't think all religions are the same. A year earlier, in 2010, the Libyan leader had been our friend, after mellowing from the worst of his fire branding. "Islam," Gaddafi told five hundred young women paid to hear him in Rome, "should become the religion of all of Europe."

We let God be any god, but not for any reason fathomable to the Christian philosophers from the first centuries after Christ, who Bishop Michael quoted in his address. Driving us isn't any thoughtful philosophy, but a multicultural ideology we've taken up more and more since the Second World War. It's pan-religious Christianity, and our numbers are falling. Along with Father Keith, only twelve parishioners sat before the bishop. My wife, eldest son, and I made up a quarter of them.

We judge for better and worse, try to save the world when it's bad, but know little beyond the walls of our homes. Cath at our Uniting church home group around about 2014 couldn't understand why Jews and Muslims fought each other in the Middle East. "They're the same religion," she said.

Jews and Muslims don't think so. The world in which we dream isn't other people's worlds. Imposing our multicultural genre upon others is as facile as other fictions in which we believe.

In France in 2009, sixty-three percent of practicing Roman Catholics believed all religions are the same. No more than sixty-four percent of the French declared themselves Roman Catholic. Less than five percent attended Mass weekly. Those proportions had fallen from eighty-one percent calling themselves Roman Catholic and twenty-seven percent attending Mass weekly in 1965.

I sympathise with some things Father Peter Kennedy did at St Mary's Roman Catholic Church, South Brisbane, such as allowing women to preach, but he also stood a statue of Buddha in the church, if church was still the right word to use. He accepted all people, whatever they thought or practiced, into the congregation, if congregation was still the right word to use. He made everything easy, so when Archbishop John Bathersby dismissed Kennedy on the third Saturday of February 2009, the congregation stood defiantly with him. They moved into the Trades Hall Council building in Peel Street.

At best, ours becomes post-Christian Christianity. At worst, we're Buddhists.

In a 2007 edition of the Dutch television programme *Network*, Bishop Martinus Muskens of Breda wanted the Dutch to learn to get on spontaneously with other cultures and behaviour patterns. It wasn't enough to get on with them. The Dutch had to get on with them intuitively, unthinkingly.

Muskens' preference was Islam. Several years earlier, he'd suggested replacing the Dutch national Christian holiday Whit Monday, the day after Pentecost, with an Islamic religious day. In 2007, he suggested Christians refer to God as "Allah" to relate better with Muslims. He claimed God didn't mind what He was called, being above such "discussion and bickering."

We've reduced the differences between religions to words, as God doesn't. Dutch Muslims hadn't asked for the change. They don't need to. We unwind our religion to become other people's religion without them needing to ask. Western multiculturalism isn't about them but about us: our vision for the world.

"Someone like me has prayed to *Allah yang maha kuasa* for eight years in Indonesia and other priests for twenty or thirty years," explained Muskens, a Roman Catholic. "In the heart of the Eucharist, God is called Allah over there, so why can't we start doing that together?"

The Indonesian word was a legacy of ancient Arabic influences, predating Islam and giving rise to Indonesia ultimately becoming Muslim. It might also have meant a minority respecting a majority, but we don't expect respect from minorities in our countries. We expect respect from majorities, at least while we're the majorities. Muskens thought Dutch people would need a century to feel comfortable with the change (by which time matters mightn't be in Dutch hands, anyway).

Muskens wasn't embracing Islam, but redefining Christianity. In

2005, he said Islam was a religion without a future, because too many aspects of it were violent.

Islam doesn't need a future with multicultural Christianity replicating it. Western Christianity has no violence (except against white racists at Gippsland Grammar School).

"Calling God 'Allah' does no justice to Western identity," retorted the chairman of the Protestant Church in the Netherlands, Gerrit de Fijter. "I see no benefit in it." (He was obviously a very unchristian fellow.)

"*Sure*," wrote Welmoet Koppenhol to a Dutch newspaper. "*Let's call God Allah. Let's then call a church a mosque and pray five times a day. Ramadan sounds like fun.*"

We surrender our rites of worship and tenets of faith for the sake of inclusion that never was God's. Nor was it ours, until after the Holocaust.

St Matthew's Anglican Church, West Pymble recognised Ramadan in 2013, with prayers every day of the month. We could really relate better with Muslims by adopting the Koran and declaring Mohammed to be Allah's one prophet.

Muslims don't equate Allah to the Christian God. What we call inclusion, other races consider intrusion.

Like those across the border in Indonesia, churches in the Malaysian Borneo states of Sabah and Sarawak had referred to God as Allah for centuries, following a practice that predated Islam. A 2010 Malaysian court ruling that a Roman Catholic newspaper could do so in the Malaysian peninsular led to Malays firebombing several churches.

Three Muslim judges in the Malaysian appeals court ruled unanimously in 2013 that only Muslims could speak of Allah. "The usage of the word 'Allah' is not an integral part of the faith in Christianity," said Chief Judge Mohamed Apandi Ali. "The usage of the word will cause confusion in the community." In 2014, Islamic authorities seized from a Christian group more than three hundred Bibles referring to God as Allah.

In European languages, God is the Christian God. A Muslim boy in one of my eldest daughter's year-nine classes swore frequently, including among his phrases, "Oh, my god!"

"I don't say, 'Oh, my Mohammed'," a rare teacher of substance corrected him. "So please don't say, 'Oh, my god'."

I'm unaware of any Muslim producing a Koran or Jew

producing a Torah without terms offensive to other religions. When they're not calling us infidels or worse, Muslims lump us with Jews among the "people of the Book." They don't lump themselves with us. Jews consider only themselves the "people of the Book."

When our parish Anglican church raffled a Volkswagen Polo car for our 2006 fête, I was among several parishioners and my friend Barry standing in shopping centres, markets, and street malls selling tickets. Western passers-by were conspicuously generous, but only a single Middle Eastern man, a Christian, bought a ticket. A Jewish man in the St Ives Shopping Village told me not to bother trying to sell tickets there, because Jews wouldn't buy tickets in a church raffle.

Jews aren't always obvious, Asians are. Very, very few among the many Asians bought tickets. East Asians gamble, but buying tickets in community raffles isn't gambling. It's donating. (Whenever I encounter people selling raffle tickets, I don't ask about the prizes. I care about who's conducting the raffle.) A Chinaman spent a long time sitting in the raffle car in our local shopping centre, carefully examining it and asking me many questions about it, but he never asked about the church, fête, or raffle. He never bought a ticket.

Equality commoditises. We commoditise religion.

Having reduced Christianity to love and all religions to being the same, the logical consequence was a ditty from Fight for Equality, to which my friend Karel referred readers of his *Facebook* computer page in 2014. "*Buddha was not a Buddhist. Jesus was not a Christian. Muhammad was not a Muslim. They were teachers who taught love. Love was their religion.*"

It was utter nonsense, even if Jesus taught love and Buddha recognised the benefit a person could gain by loving, but we redefine other religions much as we redefine ours. Even with such redefinition, Karel described his religious views as "*Abstainer.*"

Religion became unimportant when the West dropped Christian conviction, clarity, and definition. Imagining all religions being the same means there's hardly reason to bother being Christian. Nothingness Christianity offers people no reason to believe.

People truly believing their religion can't believe all religions are alike. If religions mean anything, there are distinctions between them.

Western multiculturalism presumes all religions are equally valid, but they're also mutually exclusive. At chapter 5, verse 17 the Koran declares that anyone saying Jesus, the son of Mary, is God can't be a Muslim.

Christianity believes God became a man. Islam considers that belief blasphemy. By 2009, Muslims erected a banner near the Church of the Annunciation in Nazareth quoting the passage from the Koran declaring that god does not beget, nor is he begotten, thereby denouncing Christianity.

We don't assert our faith like that. By 2012, the Wycliffe Bible Translators, the Summer Institute of Linguistics, and Frontiers all produced books they called Bibles for Muslim countries in which God was no longer the "*Father*" and Jesus no longer the "*Son*" or "*Son of God.*" That was all way too Christian.

Muslims thinking they're adopting Christianity with such books aren't. The new translations were "an all American idea with absolutely no respect for the sacredness of Scripture, or even of the growing Turkish church," protested Turkish pastor Fikret Böcek in 2012. A church leader in Bangladesh complained they gave credence to the Muslim claim that Christians were liars who changed our Bibles to deceive Muslims.

Christians of other races don't appreciate what the West is doing with Christianity, but they're not trying to be inclusive. They're not trying to appease.

Either Jesus was the Son of God, or He wasn't. Either Mohammed was God's true prophet or he wasn't. If Judaism is right, then Hinduism is wrong. If animism is right, then theism is wrong. It's inescapable for a person of faith in any religion not to believe, however courteously or not, other religions are mistaken, or dare I say wrong.

Multicultural religion yearns to be global, but isn't global and isn't religion. It's Western and it's ideology. For all faiths to be equally right or wrong, contradictory as they are, they must all be wrong. The only way to treat contradictory creeds equally, is to reject them all.

In pursuit of our postmodern, multicultural ideal, we've decided we were mistaken these past thousand and more years. The Man our forebears steadfastly called God's Son, becomes a nice boy with some fine rules for life. Christians become mortal beings who live by those rules, although there's no reason to do so. There's no reason to do anything.

Atheism is the only belief system coherent with Western multiculturalism, but that offends other races with their religions. Besides, we don't want to be challenged as to what it all means. We get along by never thinking about it. We believe everything, by which we believe nothing. All peoples are one, we think: all gods and godlessness one. Our only religious conviction is there can be no conviction. Beyond atheism and agnosticism, is nothingness: religious nihilism, the end of religion. That's all our globalist vision can be.

Whenever we try to be everything, we ultimately become nothing. Our West without racial distinctions is our world without race, if only ours. Our West without religious distinctions is our world without religion, if only ours. Multiculturalism leads us from our religion through many religions to none.

7. GOD AND JESUS

Differences between religions are much more than Jesus' divinity and the Trinity. Values and standards also differ.

Jewish historian Simon Schama based his 2013 television series *The Story of the Jews* on his book of that name. He quoted twelfth-century Jewish philosopher Judah Halevi to say Judaism was a religion of deeds, of action, Christianity a religion of faith, and Islam a religion of obedience.

"It is difficult to recognise the God of the New Testament in the god of the Koran," said Sydney's Cardinal George Pell in 2011, "and two very different concepts of the human person have emerged from the Christian and Muslim understandings of God."

Different concepts of a human person emerged with Christianity and Judaism too, but we'd put aside those differences after the Holocaust. Soon, we'd put aside all religious differences.

Born a Muslim before becoming an atheist in the Netherlands and coming to suffer the wrath of vengeful Muslims, Ayaan Hirsi Ali didn't equate Christianity and Islam. "*Churches should do all in their power to win this battle for the souls of humans in search of a compassionate God,*" she wrote in her 2010 book *Nomad*, "*who now find that a fierce Allah is closer to hand.*"

Ali was African, so we didn't pay attention. (Had a European said it, we'd have been outraged.) She believed Christianity could combat the rise of conservative Islam, but we lose that chance by insisting all religions are the same. Fierce Allah becomes indistinguishable from our compassionate God.

While there's no record Jesus married, it's inconceivable that He would have beat his wife as Mohammed beat his favourite wife Aisha after she left the house without his permission. *"He struck me on the chest which caused me pain,"* she said at book 4, number 2127 of the Book of Prayers, *Kitab Al-Salat*.

At their home in Cardiff in 2010, Sara Ege beat her seven-year-old son Yaseen to death. He'd failed to memorise portions of the Koran.

Having redefined Christianity, what used to be Christianity, with devotion to God and trust in the Bible, the West now calls fundamentalist or conservative. We do the same with Islam.

After Pakistani fashion model Qandeel Baloch said she and Mufti Qavi drank soft drinks and smoked cigarettes together during daylight hours in Ramadan in 2016, her brother murdered her. *CBS News* described the people she'd offended not as Muslims or conservative Muslims, but simply conservatives.

If we don't redefine Christianity to be without God, we redefine God. We redefine Him in our image, because we've redefined us. We're no longer European, but encompass everyone on earth. We hone in upon God loving the world, discard everything else in the Bible, and decide for ourselves what God should be: what loving must mean. We make Him postmodern, multicultural.

We've dismissed the Old Testament to redefine a New Testament without it, but for four years at our parish Anglican church, the five thirty services of a Sunday evening worked methodically through the first books of the Old, tying them to the New. Brother Ned Gerber said often we weren't just studying the easy bits. The only thing more challenging than hearing the Bible in a church hall, or in the home group that briefly replaced the services, is reading more of it elsewhere. The ticklish bits speak to how much our new visions of God aren't Biblical.

At verse 34 of Psalm 18 (and verse 35 of the Second Book of Samuel), David says God *"trains my hands for battle,"* so that *"my arms can bend a bow of bronze."* We don't fight.

In verses 21 and 22 of Psalm 139, David describes his perfect hatred of those who hate God. We don't hate.

Hatred can be Godly. Chapter 12, verse 9 of Paul's Epistle to the Romans called upon Christians to hate what is evil.

The Gospels of Matthew, Mark, and John describe Jesus entering the Temple courts of Jerusalem shortly before Passover to find moneychangers and men selling cattle, sheep, and doves. "It is written," He told them, "My house will be called a house of prayer, but you are making it a den of robbers!" Furious with them, Jesus made a whip from cord and drove them and their animals from the Temple, scattered the moneychangers' coins, and threw over their tables. "Get out of here!" he cried at the men selling doves.

The prophet Jeremiah reacted much the same way to much the same provocation, six centuries beforehand. Whether Jesus was more concerned with animal sacrifice or unrestrained commerce inside the Temple matters less than the fury with which He expelled wrongdoers. His was a wrathful intolerance of what was morally wrong, repugnant to God, and contrary to people's well-being.

Two thousand years on, Western Christians don't defend our religion, territory, or selves. When illegal immigrant Jiamei Tian vandalised the Washington National Cathedral in 2013, spokesman Richard Weinberg said the Chinese woman "deserves our prayers," in spite of calling her actions "heartbreaking" and admitting the costs of repair added to the cathedral's financial problems.

The last Saturday night in August 2014, vandals spray-painted "*Infidels!*" and "*Qur'an 3:151*" on St Bartholomew's Catholic Church, East Columbus Christian Church, and Lakeview Church of Christ in Columbus, Ohio. "*We will cast terror into the hearts of those who disbelieve for what they have associated with Allah of which he had not sent down authority,*" provides that passage in the Koran, "*and their refuge will be the fire, and wretched is the residence of the wrongdoers.*"

The vandals knew the Koran and spelt as Arabs spell, but Father Marcote couldn't contemplate Muslim crime; only Muslim victims. "Is there somebody that really believes this, that we're all infidels so they felt the need to write it all over our church?" he asked. "Is this some sort of nasty prank? Is this someone that's trying to incite people against Muslims? I mean, I don't know."

The priests at St Bartholomew's said they'd been contacted by Muslims who condemned the vandalism and offered to help remove it. By that, we judge Islam.

Our overarching image of Jesus has become the child's image: a babe in a manger. We've forgotten His righteous indignation and anger, making Him unrecognisable from the God of Joshua: a warrior who conquered cities and slayed their inhabitants. We dwell upon the meek being blessed and never feel more blessed, becoming less of a shepherd and more of a sacrificial lamb. Not simply meek, we're proud of our meekness, we little individuals.

We espouse inclusion and diversity when espousing anything else would make us pariahs, as the Jews of the Temple made Jesus a pariah. A few days after evicting those wrongdoers, Christ was crucified.

Deeming everyone equally children of God, everyone the same, raises people who hate us. We lower Christ Himself.

A warden at our parish Anglican church thought we shouldn't use an image of Jesus for our Lifeline Food Drive, 2009. In our desire to make Jesus Jewish, even mortal, Belinda presumed the image would be Middle Eastern, scaring people away.

Leaving our home, I pointed her to a picture of Christ as a child I'd recently had framed, hanging beside our front door. After my mother died, I'd found among her papers the picture prepared for the Convent of the Sacred Heart dated 1936. (She and her sister had been students of the *Religieuses du Sacré Cœur de Jésus* at the Rose Bay Junior School.) The boy Jesus' skin is lily white, His hair golden.

Belinda laughed. Multiculturalism strips us of our European heritage. It strips Jesus of being European. We've redefined God, and we've redefined His Son.

My writing isn't about the Nazarene living two thousand years ago in an obscure outreach of what was then the greatest empire on earth. There are already sixty-six, if not more, perfectly good books about Him; no disrespect, friends. My writing is about us.

Only the West pushes Jesus away from us in our imagery. We've done so since 1945.

Phill, at our family Uniting church, told me of Fijians portraying Jesus a little like a Fijian. The penultimate Sunday in September 2015, the five o'clock service showed a picture that Reverend Laurel called the African Christ: a drawing from Cameroon picturing Jesus as African. (Expecting the service to be another about asylum seekers, I'd arrived at the church praying, "Lord, give me strength." I had said I'd tend to the slide presentation.)

The more I'd learnt of the Old Testament, the more I'd been intrigued as to why God chose the Israelites for their Old Testament role: carrying His word from Genesis until Christ. Several races faithfully follow prophets or teachers from other races, but Christianity would be unique if our Saviour was of a race that didn't recognise Him.

Europeans and other Caucasians settled along much of the Mediterranean shore through Biblical times. Egypt's famous ruler Cleopatra VII, for example, was Greek. Unusually for her Ptolemaic dynasty, she learnt to speak Egyptian. Deferring to local religion as we don't imagine asking of our immigrants, she went so far as to present herself as a reincarnation of the Egyptian goddess Isis.

Many Europeans lived along the eastern Mediterranean shore through Biblical times. Until the Holocaust, we dwelt upon them. To the north of Israel, said Brother Ned Gerber the Sunday night his services reached the future king David, was a tribe of Irishmen and women. He might have meant the Galatians.

David himself was descended from Ruth, a Gentile. Chapter 16, verse 12 of the First Book of Samuel describes David as being *"ruddy, with a fine appearance and handsome features."* Chapter 17, verse 42 says Goliath *"looked David over and saw that he was only a boy, ruddy and handsome, and he despised him."*

Being ruddy is to have a fresh, reddish complexion. It can only describe a Caucasian, such as an Irishman.

There are scholars, said Ned, who believe ruddy referred to having red hair, which is still Caucasian, although chapter 5, verses 10 to 16 of the Song of Songs suggests ruddiness doesn't describe hair. *"My lover is radiant and ruddy, outstanding among ten thousand. His head is purest gold; his hair is wavy and black as a raven. His eyes are like doves by the water streams, washed in milk, mounted like jewels. His cheeks are like beds of spice yielding perfume. His lips are like lilies dripping with myrrh. His arms are rods of gold set with chrysolite. His body is like polished ivory decorated with sapphires. His legs are pillars of marble set on bases of pure gold. His appearance is like Lebanon, choice as its cedars. His mouth is sweetness itself; he is altogether lovely. This is my lover, this is my friend."*

The lover has black hair, not red, although it might be wet, dirty, or dyed. Chapter 1, verse 6 links darkness to working outside. Complicating our understanding, Lebanon was probably Phoenician. A head of purest gold being ruddy is an interesting juxtaposition, but Caucasian it is.

The fourth reference in the Bible to people being ruddy is in the Book of Lamentations, chapter 4, verse 7, describing the sons of Zion. *"Their princes were brighter than snow and whiter than milk, their bodies more ruddy than rubies, their appearance like sapphires."* God's people never appeared more European, before verse 8 talks of the punishment meted upon them. *"But now they are blacker than soot; they are not recognised in the streets. Their skin has shrivelled on their bones; it has become as dry as a stick."*

Chapter 1 of the Gospel of Matthew and chapter 3 of the Gospel of Luke describe Jesus' lineage from Abraham through David and then Joseph the husband of Mary, with Luke extending that from Abraham to Adam and God. The appearance of David is important only for what people might believe Jesus' appearance could be, because Jesus was conceived by the Holy Spirit in Mary. Her race is the sole determinant of Jesus' race. On His human side, we know nothing of the Virgin Mary's race.

There are no Biblical descriptions of Jesus. Other descriptions from that era point to a European Christ. Those descriptions need not convince Africans that Jesus was anything but African or Fijians that Jesus was not partially Fijian, but until the late twentieth century they were enough for Europeans to believe Christ was European.

Along with David and other Old Testament figures, Jesus mightn't have been racially a Jew, as we understand Jews. Jesus mightn't have been raised religiously a Jew so much as raised according to our Old Testament origins. What we think of as being Judaism wasn't codified into writing, the Mishnah and rest of the Talmud, until about 200 and 500 *anno Domini*: After Christ.

In ancient times, Israel and Judah were separate kingdoms, which might or might not have united for a period. The Old Testament Israelites were essentially a confederation of tribes, possibly twelve. The Israelite tribes shared the Old Testament cultural stream, but little else.

The Hebrew Bible and Christian Old Testament distinguish the broader group of Israelites from the narrower group of Jews, with the Jews only some of the Israelites. All Jews were Israelites. Only some Israelites were Jews. Samaritans, including the famous Good Samaritan, were Israelites but not Jews. The Jews were more synonymous with the Hebrews.

The New Testament refers to Jesus and his earliest followers as Israelites or Nazarenes, perhaps Galileans. Nazarene and Galilean were geographical, not racial, origins, as might Israelite have been.

Chapter 13 verse 43 of the Book of Acts distinguished Jews from devout converts to their religion. Both made up the congregation at the synagogue.

The Gospel of John, chapter 1, verse 11, speaks of Christ coming to His own who did not receive Him. Whether His own were the Israelites, Jews, Romans, or everyone, they did not receive Him. It was a collective sense of His own, although some individuals received Him.

The Samaritan woman in John, chapter 4, verse 9 called Jesus a Jew. Others called Him king of the Jews. He never called Himself a

Jew or king of the Jews.

In John, chapter 18, verse 36, Jesus speaks of Jews as if to say He is not a Jew. "My kingdom is not of this world," He said. "If my kingdom were of this world, then would my servants fight that I should not be delivered to the Jews, but now is my kingdom not from hence."

Modern translations often replace the reference to Jews to Jewish leaders. One commentator believed John's references to Jews means Jews who have not become Christians. In both events, we make Jesus a Jew. Jesus did not.

Jesus told Jews to give unto Caesar what was Caesar's and to God what was God's. Deferring to the Roman Empire in everything except religion, His command to love thy enemies and persecutors was a command to the Jews to love the Romans. (It wasn't a command to us to love our enemies.) Christ on the Cross pleaded for the Romans' forgiveness; they knew not what they were doing.

There is not the evidence to be certain of Jesus' race. There is evidence to be open to the possibility He was European.

Christ was the God for Rome. Perhaps He wasn't obviously born of one Caucasian race so He could be Saviour to all. It doesn't make Him any less the Saviour of the world.

The problem with God is that He hasn't changed as we changed through the twentieth century. The Jesus who'll return is no babe in a manger or sacrificial lamb.

"*With justice He judges and makes war,*" wrote John in chapter 19, verses 11 to 15 of the Book of Revelation. "*His eyes are like blazing fire, and on His head are many crowns... He is dressed in a robe dipped in blood, and His name is the Word of God. The armies of heaven were following Him... Out of His mouth comes a sharp sword with which to strike down the nations. 'He will rule them with an iron sceptre.' He treads the winepress of the fury of the wrath of God Almighty.*"

The Bible foretells Armageddon. Poor peasants can't afford to worry about it. Rich people want something to fear. Looking for Armageddon in all the wrong places, since World War II we've feared a cold war, hot war, coming ice age, computer failure, global warming, climate change, and our over-population. About the only things we refuse to fear are other races and religions, not since the Holocaust.

Chapters 17 and 18 of the Book of Revelation describe the

Whore of Babylon. Among the many interpretations of the Whore is condemnation of international super-states: globalism.

Armageddon bubbles unnoticed towards us. We mightn't know the meaning of God's Revelation to John until after the events they describe happen, for their purpose is simply that the story begun in Genesis will end, heralding a new story. Details matter less than there being an end, of sorts, before the next eon. What's allegory and what's real doesn't matter, although might matter when each prophecy unfolds. That mightn't be for thousands of years.

I used to say it might be tomorrow, until Brother Ned Gerber told me the conditions aren't met. They'll be met when the Bible has been translated into the last of the world's languages. The great commission, to which saints and others gave their lives in the first centuries after Christ and the two millennia since then, will have been fulfilled. We'd have spread the word of the risen Lord to all the peoples of earth. Mission completed.

Our mission wasn't to convert people to God, but to equip them to make choices; ours is the God of choice. Races have made their choices, even if individuals haven't. Chapter 7 of the Book of Revelation foretells a world worshipful of God comprising tribes and nations.

Ned and our parish Anglican priest Father Keith believed Armageddon will come soon. I don't know that it matters much, although if I knew it was coming tomorrow morning, I wouldn't sleep well tonight. I'd stare into the sky.

Until then, God allows us a degree of dominion over mortal earth. Biblical prophecy was a vision. It wasn't a command.

8. WHITE CHRISTIAN BURDEN

The Gospel of John, at chapter 12, and other Gospels, describes Mary pouring expensive perfume on Jesus' feet. When Judas complained that the perfume could have been sold to raise money for the poor, Jesus rebuked him. "You will always have the poor among you," said Jesus.

Thus our forebears expended great wealth glorifying Him, building beautiful churches, cathedrals, and basilicas, but we've become like Judas, chastising them for supposedly wasting resources. We proudly prefer to give everything away.

Political scientist Robert Putnam of Harvard University didn't believe in God, but with Mormon David Campbell compared religiously observant Americans with other Americans for their 2011 book *American Grace: How Religion Unites and Divides Us*. They concluded, *"for the most part, the evidence we review suggests that religiously observant Americans are more civic, and in some respects simply 'nicer'. On every measurable scale, religious Americans are more generous, more altruistic and more involved in civic life than their secular counterparts. They are more likely to give blood, money to a homeless person, financial aid to family or friends, a seat to a stranger and to spend time with someone who is 'a bit down'."*

Simon Smart, a director of the Centre for Public Christianity in Sydney, believed Putnam and Campbell's research proved the benefit of religious communities. Each individual's faith mattered less than being a religious community. *"An atheist who comes to church to support her partner,"* wrote Smart, *"will rate as well as any believer on these scores."*

Not just Christians of faith are nicer people. In Christian communities (and, dare I say, Christian countries), Christians without faith are nicer people too.

In its 2004 report *Research and Philanthropy in Australia*, the Department of Families, Community Services and Indigenous Affairs observed that religious people are more likely to volunteer, and for more hours, than other people. When I commended the role of church in communities one night at our family's Uniting church, the second Saturday in September 2012, a woman spoke proudly of the work the church was doing with indigenous communities.

"Community is good for white people, too," I told her.

The Marist Brothers, a Roman Catholic religious institute, founded the elite St Joseph's College private boarding school in Hunters Hill, Sydney in 1881. Shaun, from 2003 my colleague at Cement Australia, sent his son there. Proudly he told me the school provided several Aboriginal children with free education. Without begrudging them their opportunities, I couldn't help but wonder how many poor white children and their families would have liked the same.

The Presbyterian Church founded Knox Grammar School, at which eight students were enrolled in 2010 on financial scholarships available only to indigenous children. "The school doesn't talk very much about it," said my former classmate Peter, by then sitting on the school council.

A Jesuit founded St Ignatius College, Riverview, which I visited with some of my children in 2010. Being even more prestigious than other private schools, it offered even more bursaries and pastoral support to indigenous children: thirty in all, among fifteen hundred students.

More weights in our white man's burden, Western churchgoers are no less engrossed than other white people with saving strangers in faraway places at the expense of our own. Whether we credit our prosperity to God and providence or not, we think He wants us to share our wealth with the world.

He doesn't. There is no general Biblical equality.

Chapter 15, verse 11 of the Book of Deuteronomy acknowledges there will always be poor people. It commands Israelites to be openhanded to the poor and needy among fellow Israelites living with them in their land. There is no command to open their hand to the needy among fellow Israelites not living with them in their land or to the needy among other races.

Chapter 15 of the Gospel of Matthew and Chapter 7 of the Gospel of Mark describe Jesus' encounter with a woman who Matthew calls a Canaanite and Mark calls Greek born in Syrian Phoenicia. When she calls Him Lord, demonstrating what we would call Christian faith, Christ heals her daughter.

Any racial implications of the story are unclear and the reference to dogs, or perhaps puppies, confusing. What is clear is that Christ only healed people we would call Christians, including, it seems, those becoming Christians because of His healing. If Christ does not provide for people who are not Christians, why do Western churches provide for them?

Christian Romans and Christian Jews were fighting each other in the first century *anno Domini*, when the Apostle Paul wrote his Epistle to the Romans. Chapter 12, verse 13 called upon them to share with their fellow Christians in need, but only fellow Christians and only those in need.

This isn't equality, but charity. It doesn't cross religious lines.

Passages like chapter 2, verses 44 and 45 and chapter 4, verses 32 to 35 of the Acts of the Apostles refer to Christians sharing all they owned with each other. Sharing depends upon a shared identity, from which shared ownership and responsibility flow (as it does among Fijians and other Pacific Island tribespeople). "*All the believers were one in heart and mind,*" says Acts, chapter 4, verse 32.

In that context, Christ spoke words like "those of you who do not give up everything you have cannot be my disciples," at chapter 14, verse 33 of the Gospel of Luke. They can give everything up for their people because their people will keep them. Other people won't.

Western peoples have become individuals. We don't provide for each other. We provide for everyone else.

Our white people's burden is never more evident than in our postmodern churches, because our generosities are never more evident than under church angel wings. They make our failings most obvious.

Kat was never too passionate about her role as youth minister at our parish Anglican church. She didn't like teaching teenage boys, although her father's tolerance of homosexuality might've skewed her attitudes towards males. Only once did her passions come to the fore. She printed leaflets and affixed posters around the place advertising a woman coming into the church the last Saturday in June 2008 to talk not about God, but about what she called fair trade.

Hers was a crusade we don't need to hear. The South Asian's presentation trumpeting herself and her business was more tiresome than any sermon had been, but hearing was the price we paid for afternoon tea. The price was too high. Our only respite was the first few times she denigrated a competitor association also preaching fair trade. Their sectarianism was greater than any I'd seen between Christian denominations.

Parishioners buying tea, coffee, and chocolates from her would pay more than we paid at the stores so the growers of Sri Lanka and other dark-skinned countries would receive more money, although much less than the extra money we paid. I couldn't help but wonder how many Australian farmers being bundled from their land would've liked such kindness. Deregulating the New South Wales dairy industry took money from dairy farmers and their communities to benefit Sydney shoppers and supermarkets. Most of the world values foodstuffs less than industrial products. We care when it affects other races.

The only people who might help poor white people are rich white people, but we're busy helping everyone else. *"Doing training for volunteer refugee work this weekend,"* wrote my faithful old school friend Roy on his Facebook computer page, the third Thursday of November 2011. *"Hoping to make a real difference and overcome the trend to myopic me focus the world is pushing."*

We assume the West is the world, and that the alternative to our individualism is saving other races. Poor white people rarely rate a mention.

What became our family's Uniting church first attracted my wife's attention when our local newspaper mentioned that a donkey would carry children around the church forecourt that coming Palm Sunday, 2007. Inside the church, prayers and noticeboards became crammed with thoughts and deeds to help indigenous people, immigrants, and poor people around the world: people unable to get there for the donkey. A handful of parishioners also helped a mother's group in Bidwill, I think it was, but only once have I heard mention of it.

Shortly before Christmas 2013, my wife and I attended the service of seven (abridged from the traditional nine) lessons and carols. Reverend Laurel's sermon spoke less of Jesus than an Afghan girl Malala, campaigning for Muslim girls' education. Amidst our fixation with everything but God, even at Christmas time, Laurel wanted Australians to offer more refugees a place to belong. I wondered why poor outcast white people imagined churches offering them such a place.

The church sent money and cans of food to the Asylum Seeker Centre in Newtown. Parishioners collected some of the asylum seekers in community detention and brought them to the church some Monday nights to play sport. (Community detention can't have been too detaining.) They found one refugee a job in October 2013, but the job required a forklift driving certificate. Parishioners paid the cost of him getting it.

I thought of asking if they helped Australians as much and they do when the opportunity arises, but we seek out other races as they seek out us. Nor did I mention the unknown Australian who missed out on a job and possibly a forklift driving certificate.

I learnt the refugee was Muslim by a parishioner's remark that he would be transporting wine. Phill (forever the optimist) thought that meant he was ideal for the job. Our churchgoers' benevolence in deed and spirit can seem boundless, but with each Christian charity's resources finite, every beneficiary from another religion is one less from ours.

More worrying was wondering how that Muslim with his forklift would react if he ever didn't get something he wanted. Our munificence isn't turning recipients towards Christ. We're just adding to their sense of entitlement.

Without nationalism or other tribalism joining benefactors and beneficiaries, sharing creates a sense of entitlement. Able-bodied people thus choose not to work, in spite of the rule Paul cited in his Second Epistle to the Thessalonians, chapter 3, verse 10: "*The one who is unwilling to work shall not eat.*"

In his 1952 book *Mere Christianity*, Englishman C.S. Lewis wrote that Scripture suggested there "*would be no passengers or parasites*" in a Christian society. No race in history has done more to create passengers and parasites than we have.

Of one Christian charity operating in western Sydney, Muslims took about eighty percent "*of their Charity's Christmas resources, ranging from Christmas hampers (special Halal ones, mind you) to gifts for the kids (that are normally opened on the spot),*" wrote Andy of a friend working there, while commenting upon a newspaper article in December 2012. The Lakemba mosque had issued a fatwa against Christmas after Sheikh Yahya Safi, the head imam, told Muslims during Friday prayers they should refuse everything to do with Christmas and New Year. Wishing people a Merry Christmas was a sin.

The fatwa wasn't a problem, but publishing it on the Facebook website the next morning was a public relations blunder, when public relations mattered. Muslim community leaders hurriedly dismissed it. The mosque blamed it on a youth worker copying the text from another Islamic website, as if that meant we could ignore it.

Instead of defending Christmas, journalist Anthony Sharwood explained why the fatwa was unnecessary. "*The thing about Christmas in Australia,*" he wrote, "*as in much of the western world, is that it transcends religion. It is a cultural event as much as anything, a time for family and relaxation.... But the festival has by and large, become a celebration of togetherness and giving which happens to have a Christian title.*"

That was to say, we're dealing with Christmas already. Muslims don't need to do anything. The most common responses to Western peoples being asked what Christmas and Easter means to them have nothing to do with God. The West removed our religion, while we ceased spending time with our families. We've made Christmas another chance to give things away.

Western churchgoers don't imagine confining our charity to fellow Christians any more than we imagine confining it to our race. We might even like our beneficiaries being of other races and religions, for what it says about us. We persist helping them whatever they think of us, and whatever we think of ourselves in spite of it.

Our local Baptist church stood along the street from the preschool my children attended. Like other white congregations, the parishioners were lovely, good hearted, and old. Their children didn't attend church as they did, although the church hosted a girls' brigade unit that brought my two elder daughters there each Tuesday night.

My family was in the church hall because my nine-year-old second daughter had volunteered to dress into her bright blue and white girls' brigade uniform and wait on tables through a Saturday market. She was like that: serving tea, coffee, and pikelets. Aside from the girls of the girls' brigade, few children were there. At least one of the items left unsold, a small child's scooter, appeared the next day among items dumped in donation outside our parish Anglican church opportunity shop.

The largest photograph in the Baptist church wasn't of clergy or parishioners but of Shefali Kisku, who attended the Ishurdi Hostel in Bangladesh. The colourful image gave no hint of her age, but born on the eighteenth day of March 1991, she would've been seventeen years old by the time I saw her grinning, with her modest bright orange and white dress hanging loosely over much of her long white slacks. Kindly old parishioners of that Sydney suburban church sent her money, presumably receiving reports every so often of her progress to womanhood.

Also receiving money were children with disabilities in Cambodia. The church's missionary union organised a mini market to send them wheelchairs, pay their school fees, and buy them medicine.

I was again in the hall early December, for the last night of girls' brigade. I noticed, although they seemed to have long been there, the posters on the board at the far end of the hall. Pictured there was Nirma Hajong, also in Bangladesh. Her date of birth was the twentieth day of September 2000, so the caption quoting her words was already obsolete. "*I am 7 years old and am in year 2 at school.*" By the time I saw her photograph, she was eight years old. She might die an old woman before the caption changed. Her hobbies were home duties.

"*We are Hindu believers,*" the little girl wrote, or said, "*but we go to church on Christmas Day with our neighbours.*" Saying so seemed sensible, and I dare say elicited a warmer smile in the decent old folk of the church than the cynical chuckle it raised in me. For enough money each month, I'd go pretty well anywhere once a year too. She'd not needed to mention church for the money to keep coming, but she and the child sponsorship organisers wouldn't have known white Christians as well as I knew us.

Our money helps, but the logs in our eyes are much bigger than any specks in theirs. We live solitarily, even pointlessly, but comfortably, whatever the consequences. The peoples we're helping are poor to be sure, but they're young peoples. When we've become too aged to keep helping them, I'm not sure who will, or if our help meant much anyway, except to us. They mightn't care that we've gone.

The traits and values dictated in one place aren't readily suspended in others. The chief executive of Australia's largest supermarket company reputedly tried to drive a small supermarket out of business by visiting a mutual supplier's premises and illegally telling the supplier it could cease supplying his supermarkets if it continued supplying the small competitor. Unfettered by law or morality, the company did almost everything it could to maximise its profits. Yet in June 2011, that chief executive long retired proudly told St Ives Baptist Church of the company helping Aborigines by not selling them alcohol.

We compete without compromise with each other. We offer charity to everyone else.

The supermarket executive was also a past parishioner at the Anglican church in which my elder daughters and younger sons were christened. The family minister there invited volunteers to lead a new children's group, which my wife came to the church to discuss. Colin intercepted her out the front with its purpose-built ramp, quietly ushering her to a back entrance where he assisted her lugging her double pram with two toddlers and new baby up a set of rickety stone steps. Thus he ensured they weren't seen or heard by people meeting in the hall, who insisted upon their right to exclusive use of church premises. My wife asked no questions, but later consulted the parish newsletter to learn the group's name: the Friendship Circle.

We stopped attending the church after a woman whisked away the plate from which our children were taking tea biscuits, bland and dry as they were. "They are only for adults," she told them.

Some years earlier, the supermarket executive reputedly led a group of parishioners angry that their priest challenged them to help poor people. (Helping Aborigines would've been fine, but not poor white people.) The parishioners might've felt the priest was speaking down to them, which nobody likes anymore. They fired the priest, and wiped all but the briefest reference to his name from the church history, titled *Living with Stones*. We bought the book; he's hardly mentioned. Perhaps the parishioners only gave God a warning.

9. BELONGING

At the core of our civilisation the West now rejects weren't merely the cultures in which we've lost confidence, the rules we've come to resent, the mores we've come to malign, or even the salvation we desperately need. It's the belonging we individuals crave.

"The word religion derives from the Latin word 'religare', which means 'to bind together'," wrote Martha Beck in 2008. (She called herself a life coach: a nice term for someone paid to tell people what to do, a priest for people who choose what they hear.) *"As you go along your spiritual search, observe the long-term effect of every doctrine and practice that comes your way. If it breaks, shatters, or destroys, it's not religion – it's absolutism. That drug'll kill you. Real religion, by definition, makes things whole again. It heals."*

Feelings, we want. Truth, we've made less important.

"One of the important functions of religion is to give people a sense of belonging to a moral community based on religious faith," said sociologist Chaeyoon Lim of the University of Wisconsin-Madison, after he and Robert Putnam published their report *Religion, Social Networks, and Life Satisfaction* in 2010. "This community, however, could be abstract and remote unless one has an intimate circle of friends who share a similar identity. The friends in one's congregation thus make the religious community real and tangible, and strengthen one's sense of belonging to the community."

A congregation might well do more to keep people in church than all the scholars and preachers, but the Western churches flourishing are huge ones, where we stand beside strangers embroiled in personal emotions, glancing at them only to see how much money they tend to the offertory. (With direct debiting from bank accounts, we don't even have that.) It's the belonging of a crowd, not much better than none. Single-person faith means our faith is no reason to identify with others, not even others sharing our faith. We're estranged from each other when we stand before God, and in the rest of our solitary lives.

We might have circles of friends, even intimate ones, but few of us have Christian or other communities: Christianity without church. We've no connection to people beside us in church or in a shop selling karma and crystals.

Western peoples keeping the faith aren't too good with belonging. We identify with Christianity, even consume bits of it, particularly in America and Australia, but have lost our broader belonging. We're individually Christian, not citizens of a country or race. Losing our countries erodes God's house on earth, but we don't dwell upon losing so many from our own: our people who could've had faith had our countries endured, but who live and die unsaved.

The Sacred Heart church in Pymble came to call itself a parish centre. Leaving a tall Spanish-style church on the Pacific Highway, it built new premises in a small side street. Lying low, the parish centre's bland brick walls were reclusive, disappearing. The only sharp lines were roofs to deflect rainwater. If they dreamed of reaching up to heaven as our cathedrals and churches used to reach, they weren't reaching far. Not quite ashamed, the parish centre wasn't confident either. It might've been trying just to survive, hang on, and feared that if it showed its face to passers-by, then it might die.

Turramurra Uniting Church came to call itself a worship centre. Its new building also lacked a steeple.

Without the authority and togetherness of church, parish and worship centres are private places. We have company, but only for as long as we're there. Each of us sits alone.

They no less than everything else are no longer part of a country. Away from services, the doors are locked.

The church in Mortdale at which our friend Jenna married Stuart was the model of a Western multicultural church. The brick building was bland, without cultural style. The postmodern walls, outside and inside, were bare, without art, sculpture, or colour, aside from a huge banner near the street portraying words like "*love*" and "*community*," picturing old white people and a young myriad of races, all merrily smiling. Stuart is Australian, but his two groomsmen were Chinese and Arab.

Hidden in a church garden was an old stone pedestal presented to or from the Red Cross, I think. On a wall in the narthex hung a dark wooden board as once hung in a church to list the hymns sung that day or evening, but the board was empty. So incongruous they were, they reeked of being token keepsakes from a church of Christendom culture long closed, perhaps by then an accountant's office or funeral parlour.

The only bright items on the narthex wall were photographs of smiling church personnel and notices of coming church activities, among which was a single breath of Western culture and indeed of culture at all. Christmas was coming and the church was organising evenings for children to put together gingerbread houses.

The wedding service was brief, with two songs (one of which was nice) instead of hymns, but Reverend Dennis' address offered a few small affronts to Western individualism. He had the insensitivity to rebuke Western transience. He also put God at the centre of marriage, following from people of faith putting God at the centre of our lives. It was old-style Christianity with conviction in the midst of multiculturalism, defying the world we created outside and inside our churches. Our private, individual religions seemed rather small.

Stuart and Jenna are more than one life, but still only two lives. They're far, far less than a people.

We have the same lack of concern as the faithless for the consequence upon our compatriots of what they believe. The Australian Broadcasting Corporation managing director Mark Scott was a Christian of faith, who let Radio National cancel *The Religion Report* from its programmes. He had his faith. That was enough.

If we evangelise, it's because we feel called to evangelise. We don't care if we succeed, so long as we try.

We have little engagement with our people, except on our terms; the choices that matter are ours. Our faith, fulfilment, and security mean everything, but only to us. To everyone else, they mean nothing at all.

The best thing is never to mention them. A fellow soccer and school parent with the Christian name Scott, who'd coached my youngest son's first soccer team, was a Christian of faith, but I only learnt it from the Facebook website. (We learn more about people we meet from their computer pages than we glean from weak conversation.) It wasn't so much what Scott marked as being his religious views, for that was just "*Yes!*" His profile picture appeared to be of him playing a harmonica in church, with dark glasses covering his eyes. I learned of his faith because one of the pages of which he was a fan was the Centre for Public Christianity.

Christianity was never less public than it is in our multicultural West. I suppose I felt a little snubbed that he declined my invitation to befriend me on the site, although sensible people have many sound reasons not to accept every invitation they receive. My school reunion had been reason for me to look at the site and Scott's name and picture appeared at the side of the screen, but he became concerned when I told him that people could see his profile. Liking to maintain barriers between him and the people he managed at work, he didn't want them learning anything personal about him.

The person to whom he reported might've felt the same way. Soon afterwards, Scott was fired from his job.

Christianity is no reason to fetter our economic individualism. David was another Christian of faith, whose son Damien was also at school with my youngest son. He and his wife suffered the cruel loss of a daughter stillborn and my wife was pleased to be among the people preparing meals for their family, leaving them in an Esky cooler outside their home. Yet, when David read that trade unions were planning to use new workplace laws becoming effective on New Year's Day 2010 to push for conditions at work to become family friendly, he wrote on his Facebook computer page that it seemed like an excuse to reduce working hours and so productivity.

Renegade Reverend Fred Nile (an elected New South Wales legislative councillor) had a broad sense of belonging: to his people and country. He organised a residents meeting in response to a proposal to establish a Muslim school in Camden. So loudly I couldn't help but overhear, at a cocktail party in a northern Sydney parliamentarian's home in December 2007, former legislative councillor John Ryan complained to my friend Patrick that Nile had involved himself in the matter. Atheists like Patrick were content to believe God isn't real, without seeing harm in people of faith. Ryan considered himself an evangelical Christian.

Ryan wasn't interested in the rights and feelings of the people of Camden. He felt no belonging with them.

We don't side with Christians. A week into October 2014, apparently working its way through every religion except Christianity, Gordon Uniting Church declared from its Pacific Highway noticeboard: *"Buddhists Welcome Here."*

Relentlessly trying to embrace other religions while other religions don't embrace each other leads us into a muddle. In July 2013, Britain's Methodist Conference passed Notice of Motion 201, wanting a report on whether to join the Muslim Boycott, Divest, and Sanction Movement against Israel. The conference cited the call of the prophet Micah at chapter 6, verse 8 of the Book of Micah to *"do justice, to love kindness and to walk humbly with your God."* Micah never imagined God's people siding with another religion to pressure Israel out of existence.

Any vestiges of the West fade away. While living in Mosman, my eldest son attended St Clement's Anglican Church. It became the Village Church early in 2023. The last Wednesday in November 2024, long after he left Mosman, he recalled the new name as *"something meaningless."*

In 2022, my childhood church St Paul's Anglican Church amalgamated with St Andrew's Anglican Church to form Wahroonga Anglican Church. At the St Luke's Presbyterian Church fete in November 2024, I learnt that sometime since my family and I attended a Scottish service there, the church had become Roseville Presbyterian Church.

The saints might not have been European, but dedicating our churches with their anglicised names was part of our British heritage. Deleting the saints, our churches delete our heritage: a little something of the churches' Britishness. At least those churches continued calling themselves churches.

While at school, my middle son and youngest daughter attended a youth group at St Matthew's Anglican Church, West Pymble of a Friday night. Later, in June 2021, it merged with All Saints' Air Force Memorial Church, West Lindfield, which my family knew from a fete we attended there. Instead of naming the merged body for a saint, or for all saints, it became the racially and religiously ambiguous North Light.

In August 2021, the merged body conducted a 'Kingdom Citizens' series. In its words, *"we continue thinking about how Jesus subverts cultural expectations of who is 'in' with God."* I did not know what that meant.

My family and I also attended services in St Martin's Anglican Church, Killara. In November 2023, it and St Peter's Anglican Church, East Roseville became Living Hope Anglican. Combining churches masks their decline. (It also aids the sale of valuable land, like that in Killara, Penny remarked to me the first Sunday in December 2023.)

Our churches take up names that might have Biblical bases (as Living Hope does, the reverend insisted to me, the day before Anzac Day, 2024), but those obscure bases are not unique to Europe or to Christianity. Instead, they exude abstract notions of spirituality and personal discovery rather than Europe or Christianity. To avoid excluding any race or religion, they exclude all races and religions. Western churches, like the West, are devolving into a cultureless, irreligious nothingness.

Throughout the West, our churches are becoming cafeterias, antique stores, and magic shops. When Tom, the senior minister from St Philip's Church, Turramurra, went cycling through Brittany years earlier, he saw the churches boarded up and derelict. Centuries earlier, France had been called the Eldest Daughter of the Roman Catholic Church. What stirred with great hymns became hollows in still air.

Individuals don't care. We observe.

Christianity dwindles and withers in Christendom, but losing our churches matters no more to us than losing our countries. The decline of Western Christianity is symptomatic of the end of our collective identities; the dissolution of our churches mirrors the dissolution of our countries.

The West rejected religion when we rejected belonging: racism and nationalism. Western peoples ceased attending church not for ceasing to be Christian, but for ceasing to be peoples.

10. OTHER PEOPLE'S CHURCHES

Tom, who'd seen those empty churches in Brittany, was a friend of Bruce, my childhood neighbour. Bruce was an earnest fellow, becoming an economist, who thought carefully before speaking and as he spoke. He was also a devout Christian, who resigned from his banking career to become a missionary. Not for him the wilds of Africa, with a bark roof overhead, dirt floors, rain for running water, and no electricity. He'd take no risk of cannibals boiling him in a pot. No, Bruce wanted to be a missionary in the south of France.

"Hell," I said, "even I'd be a missionary in the south of France!" I could lie on the lazy sandy beaches, drink cocktails brought by waitresses, wear sunglasses to shade my eyes from the sunny sparkles reflecting on the water, and talk about God.

As life transpired, Bruce and his German wife went to Muslim Kazakhstan. The formerly communist country was nominally a secular state with a third of the people Christian, principally Russians who'd come to run everything and eastern Germans deported there after World War II, but Muslim majorities don't allow Christian missionaries. (They're much like the West, in that respect.) Bruce and Edith gave up their years and donors' money to teach the English language to Kazakhs.

We have much to learn from other races about identity, loyalty, and conviction, whatever their religion. They believe what they used to believe, or don't dwell upon what they don't. (We can't learn anything from Buddhists about being self-absorbed that we don't already know.) Whether they learn anything from us, is up to them.

We're the only race on earth more interested in promoting our religion among other races, than trying to keep our people on board. Instead of saving the West, we're saving everyone else. The absent Church evangelises elsewhere, while the faith of our people falls. Our euphemism for evangelism among Muslims is outreach, but if Christmas carols create offence in our countries, they're piffling aside the rudeness of Christianity in theirs.

Western church missionaries are much like faithless Western aid agencies, helping and entertaining the impoverished of other races instead of our poor. We trip around Asia, Africa, and Latin America teaching school, building homes, and caring for the sick. The arrogance of our good works evangelism imagines our example quietly turning a few appreciative others towards God, converting some of them to Christianity, when their races long ago chose otherwise.

Saving souls, but not ours, we think opening our lands to other races improves their chances of becoming Christians. Much as primitive people suddenly seeing European missionary's material wealth formed cargo cult religious movements, our affluence might tempt them, although their alleged conversions might last no longer after they obtain refugee status or residency permits than do those of prisoners in gaols with high dispositions to finding God, before facing parole boards. We equate repentance with regret – regret for having been caught.

Other races don't enthuse about lost white people adopting their religions as we enthuse for the few from other races claiming ours. Desperate for new believers, we're keen to champion them coming from other faiths or from none; we don't discriminate. They're crude recruits, but better than none, while our race stays away.

Western Christians finding the handful of immigrants turning to Christ ignore not only the overwhelming majority who maintain their foreign faiths. It ignores the far more numerous white people abandoning churches that seem completely uninterested in them. The people who might save Western Christianity are Western.

No Australian visiting our parish Anglican church excited Jacqui B as much as a Muslim Arab entering the penultimate Sunday in May 2015. Two days later, still unable to contain herself, she commandeered the prayer time among Scripture teachers at our local primary school to talk about him. Later that Tuesday morning, she bombarded Father Keith in his office with her exuberance. The Arab hadn't become a Christian, but never had Jacqui felt more humbled (and we do like feeling humbled) than she'd felt to hear him telling her that Christians are the nicest people.

"We are," I told my wife, telling me about it that afternoon. "We're the most generous people on earth. It doesn't matter how many of our people you kill, we'll still put our arms around you, give you a big hug, and give you more."

We're not embracing our race. Jacqui refused to travel to working-class suburbs for her accreditation to remain a Scripture teacher. "I'm not going to Blacktown!" she declared to her fellow teachers.

Brother Ned Gerber, whose Benedictine order operated a hospital in Africa, embraced Africans with enthusiasm that would've made Africans blush. Not just spending time with Africans in Africa, America, and Australia, he brought to Sydney to teach us about faith an African primate (a religious primate, not a gorilla).

In spite of Ned recently agreeing with me that Western individualism was the greatest bar to Western people being Christian, he was most passionate telling my wife that the high percentage of Chinese living in our suburb made it imperative to bring them into our parish Anglican church. Denying Australian identity, he, Kat, and Diane promoted their Forward in Faith International, Australasia conference titled 'Upholding the Gospel as part of the Asian world' in 2012.

I shouldn't have been surprised. When reviewing an early draft of this book, Ned deleted my words about other races: "*Whether they want to learn anything from us is up to them.*" We're preoccupied with preaching to others, although we lack the conviction to say very much. We're much too polite to proselytise.

Communities in church are like those without. When other races go to church, they prefer their own.

A rare person to refer to Asians not integrating with us as a problem (or, indeed, to mention it at all) was the reverend at St Martin's Church, coincidentally also called Martin. He'd sent his children to school in another part of Sydney so they could be better prepared for life than he thought they'd be in racially homogenous Killara. He'd wanted them to school with Asian children.

Within only a few years, they could've remained in Killara for that. By 2014, the Chinese comprised their own congregation at the church, gathering under the auspices of the Philadelphia Anglican Church and conducting bilingual services (which didn't mean English and Chinese, but Cantonese and Mandarin) from eleven thirty each Sunday morning. Their minister was Carson Wu.

Immigrants that integrate with us don't remain when opportunities to be with their own arise. At the Anglican church in which our elder daughters and younger sons were baptised, our Chinese friend Linda was a great help when we owned only one car and that car required service or repairs. She took our eldest son to the school he attended with her son, and brought him home again afterwards. She moved along from that church before we did, because she felt increasingly uncomfortable being a rare Asian there. Married to a white Australian, she wanted to attend a church, another Anglican church, with more Asians.

In August 2021, with Sydney in lockdown due to the Wuhan virus, the director of music resigned after thirteen years at our parish church. The Chinese organist remained.

There was no word of the church hiring a new director of music, but in September 2021, our parish priest's weekly message wrote that "*I have lodged an advertisement with MOORE College regarding having a student for next year. The job description includes that the applicant be bilingual, Mandarin & English. This person would be seen to assist in the relaunching of the Play Group Ministry. This person would also be involved with Sunday duties.*"

Years earlier, our parish church appointed a Chinese woman to operate the play group with visions of her bringing in immigrants from all races. She led the play group to be solely Chinese. Chinese only wanted to attend Chinese church services.

White people imagine immigrants coalescing with us and with each other. They do not. Retaining their connectedness and self-respect, they coalesce by race.

We used to do so too. We became and remain alone.

Our parish priest's weekly message went onto mention Afghanistan. "*There are disturbing News Reports flowing out of Afghanistan regarding the retribution being cruelly carried out on the families who are accused of assisting America and her allies. The brutality of sections of the Taliban is shocking.*"

Never missing an opportunity, our parish priest asked parishioners: "*Will you continue to pray for their safety and their possibility of escaping Afghanistan as refugees?*" Not content with welcoming refugees already in the world, our churches wanted more.

At the parish council meeting in March 2023, our parish priest feared war between Australia and China. His stated fear was not

Australian deaths, but that Chinese parishioners at the church might suffer prejudice.

To give our children time at church with other children, my family for some years attended Roseville Uniting Church of a Sunday evening. There, Phill dismissed the idea that Christianity is the religion of Europe. "The Koreans wouldn't say that," he remarked, late in 2013.

My point was the reason white people condemn Christianity as we don't condemn other religions, although that was of no interest to Phill. He wanted all races to feel free to participate.

Whenever we're inclusive of all peoples on earth, we end up abandoning our own. Christianity being our religion doesn't keep it from being other races' religion, but it isn't Korea's heritage as it is ours. Koreans will decide whether it's their future.

St Margaret's Uniting Church was sold to a Korean congregation. Where Australians had drunk tea and eaten biscuits, hang signs in Korean I can't read. Margaret is no longer the matron saint. I'm no longer at home there.

Reverend Les Pearson had no qualms about race as Denistone East Uniting Church prepared in 2010 to conduct its last service in English. Denistone was "delightfully Asianised," he said, welcoming the new colonisations as we no longer cherish our old. In our gleeful surrender, the church once Christendom we built would become exclusively Korean.

Elderly parishioner Ron Hoffman accepted the change, but would miss his church. "It's a very caring church," he said. "Everyone knows everybody. I will always remember its heyday where the Sunday school had three hundred children, our youth group had seventy teenagers, and at Christmas you couldn't fit everybody into this hall."

We allow church congregations to move seamlessly from our race to others, without noticing the change. If we notice it, we welcome it, much as we do with our countries.

At Easter 2012, Christian Research Association director Philip Hughes explained why Asians and not Australians fill Australian churches in terms of our new Western individualism. Asians are "joiners," he said. "They like face to face community gatherings and join in. They are not so individualistic as Anglos."

Other races fill places of worship because they retain their collective identities: family, race, and nation. They retain their sense of community.

Hughes also linked Asians in church with their respect for authority much rarer among Europeans. "They are far more willing than most Anglos to accept the strong authority system they find in Pentecostal and other charismatic churches, which are a good stepping point away from traditional Chinese churches."

Presbyterian minister Richard O'Brien spoke of Buddhist Asians beginning with religion and some taking up Christianity as a preferable option, while white people challenge religion altogether. "People from Buddhist cultures question which is the right way to go, whereas people from the West ask 'Can we trust the Bible?'" The West was no longer looking for the right way to go.

Buddhism is an adjunct to racial identities for its Asian adherents. For Western devotees without racial identities, it's more than another mantra. (White people hardly need any more reason to do whatever we want to do.)

Particularly adept at picking up the language of the country in which he was living, at least when talking to people of other races, my Hong Kong Chinese friend Ted complimented multiculturalism on Sydney's suburban North Shore. "It's multiracial," I told him, "but hardly multicultural." Three South Asians, two Chinese married to Australians, and a half-Filipina girl sat with us in our parish Anglican church, although the half-Filipina girl soon left.

I was wrong. Mine was a narrow construction of what constitutes culture, missing far more than I, at the time, noticed.

Christians from other races aren't as accommodating as white Christians are. Long after we befriended them, I learnt Ayaz was born a Muslim, who'd become Christian because of his fellow South Asian Essy, whom he ultimately married. Muslims renouncing their faith are rare events. Rarer still are them becoming Christian.

Without the church we shared, we'd have never become friends. When Essy heard my wife was unwell, she invited our elder children to play with their younger children, with whom they were at school. Yet she didn't let her daughter come to my second daughter's tenth birthday party while she and Ayaz were busy attending another church, refusing the kind offer of a friend whose daughter was coming to the party to bring her daughter too. Mere faith didn't meld us together.

I can't imagine what Ayaz and Essy would've been without their new faiths or with their old, any more than I could imagine the same of my wife or me without ours, but theirs wasn't Western Christianity. They were resolute in their beliefs, clear and unequivocal, without accommodating others. Theirs was an Asian Christianity, with devotions to God and their race and culture, not to everyone else. Their religion they practiced with exclusion.

Our local public school taught yoga as sport. Ayaz and Essy refused to let their daughter participate because yoga is Eastern mysticism, as I hadn't realised. Our parish Anglican church hall hosted yoga too.

Ayaz and Essy didn't just object to alcohol being served at the annual church fête and after evensong and some funerals (as many Americans of faith would also object). They refused to attend church fêtes again. They never came to evensong, anyway. I'm not sure if they refused to attend funerals.

Like us, they saw the first birthday party for their daughter's friend Chantelle's dog Bella as being indulgent. Unlike us, they barred their daughter from attending. I told our second daughter that, like much of my experiences in life, there are times she should simply observe the wackiness around.

Ours isn't a Christian loss of religious and other cultural conviction. It's a Western one.

"The custom and culture of Samoa two hundred years ago did not include Christianity," said American Samoan attorney Charles Ala'ilima in 2020. "But guess what? Nobody would say now that the custom and culture of Samoa does not include Christianity." Laws protected the territory's customs and cultures while they evolved, he said.

"At the end of the day, we are so proud of who we are," said Tisa Fa'amuli. "We love who we are, and we don't want to change that."

The American Samoa government reported that every Samoan was Christian. Local leaders enforced prayer curfews, by which village police ring bells at six o'clock signalling that it was time to go inside for family prayer.

Christianity becomes a donut faith, flourishing among some of the races to whom we took it, dying among ours. We survived communism better than we're surviving individualism. We're not surviving multiculturalism at all. Whether Christianity really blossoms among other races or they take what we give them and meld a little of our ritual with their senses of togetherness and authority, I don't know. We're just letting our religion fare a little better among them than it fares among us.

I think it was the Uniting church in Tryon Road, Lindfield, whose last dedicated minister resigned because the Uniting Church embraced homosexuality around the turn of the new millennium, although the Uniting Church allowed individual Uniting churches to make their own decisions. Certainly, that church lost parishioners over time, while Koreans came to carry out their services as they wished, oblivious to what white people did.

Much like other Western authorities, our ecclesiastical authorities welcome other races replacing us in our churches. They encourage it.

Reverend Laurel told my wife that the Uniting Church pushed the last white parishioners from the Tryon Road church off to the church across the Pacific Highway at Lindfield. The Uniting Church respected the Koreans wanting the church to be theirs, without foisting diversity on them.

The last Sunday in February 2013, Warwick at our family's Uniting church (the husband of the children's minister) delighted in the Uniting Church (of all churches) forcibly ushering out the last members of an aged Australian congregation to make way for four hundred Tongans. He said the Tongans would breathe new life into the congregation, as if the congregation was something other than its people.

"I sympathise with them," I told him, of the old congregation. "A church isn't just a space. When they go, the congregation is dead. The Tongans are something else altogether."

The church became Tongan. It ceased being Australian. Our churches become the property of other races.

Warwick might have been an Australian citizen but he was not British, as the aged congregation would have been. He was Dutch.

Like Laurel, Warwick felt great deference to collective identities for other races, but felt no collective identity with his own. The pan-European identity we imagined when we opened Australia to other Europeans never arose outside churches. It never arose within them.

A year later, Warwick and his wife separated. She too was British, as was the community minister.

Like the Koreans, I'm not interested in the religions other races choose or the cultures in which they express them, provided they don't affect us. I'm only interested in the religion Western peoples choose, even if other white Christians are not.

11. CHURCH AND STATE

Another new idea Thomas Jefferson espoused for Virginia and then America through the eighteenth century to escape some of the complications he'd seen in Europe (particularly France) was to separate church and state. It was a separation of structure protecting each from the other, but also ensuring Christians of all denominations were equally eligible for public office.

The first Europeans in Europe to separate church and state were the French. Roman Catholicism ceased to be the state religion with the 1789 revolution, although was again the state religion through various imperial periods of the nineteenth century. Church and state weren't formally separated until 1905.

Article 13 of the 1918 communist Russian constitution separated church and state *"in order to ensure…freedom of conscience."* The 1924 constitution of the new multicultural, communist Union of Soviet Socialist Republics didn't. Article 124 of the 1936 Soviet constitution separated church and state as well as church from schools, in a distinction of which we've lost track in the West.

Separating church and state isn't law in most countries, not even in the West. In the United Kingdom, the church is the state. The reigning monarch, the Defender of the Faith, heads the Church of England. Britain prohibited Roman Catholics and their spouses ascending to the throne, but never thought to prohibit Jews or people of other religions when such religions were unimaginable among European royalty.

The most practical effect of Britain's official state religion being the Church of England is in the designation of public holidays. (It's one thing for the West to give up on God. It's quite another to give up public holidays.)

Our failure to distinguish religions maligns our own. Britain's National Secular Society made much of political scientist Steven Kettell's 2013 paper 'State Religion and Freedom: A Comparative Analysis,' heading its report: 'Where there is state religion, there is less freedom.' Kettell advocated a secular state, but tucked down in the report was mention that the particular religion mattered. *"Whilst according to one index used, just one of those countries with an Islamic state religion was considered free, according to another there was no free country with Islam as its state religion. By contrast, the vast majority of free countries with a state religion were Christian (i.e. Roman Catholic, Protestant, or Orthodox)."*

In his 2011 article 'Thou shalt separate Church and State,' political scientist Dean Jaensch blamed combining church and state for the Christian crusades to the Holy Land beginning almost a thousand years earlier (unconcerned or unaware those Crusades were self-defence from marauding Muslim Turks), the Spanish Inquisition five hundred years earlier (unconcerned or unaware the Spaniards were reacting to centuries of Muslim occupation and Jewish intrusion we'd now call multiculturalism), and the massacre of the Huguenots more than four hundred years earlier, as well of course as the Jewish Holocaust.

The second time I published my comments on a news website was to say the Holocaust said more about the dangers of combining atheism and state. Among the pointless diatribes I provoked, Chris L accused me of bringing up Hitler to denigrate atheism. Citing the Holocaust to criticise Christianity is fine, but not to criticise atheism.

The Spanish Inquisition weeded out Muslim influences left behind by Moor invaders and Jewish influences left behind by Jewish intruders, restoring Christianity to its European form. (We could do with that now.)

In our age, we don't use torture. We prefer derision. Our New Western Inquisition weeds out Christianity.

Jaensch also blamed combining church and state for the 2001 Muslim attacks on America, although I'd have thought that if America were to blame for being attacked, then it was for separating church and state so completely since World War II, but apparently not.

Campaigning in 1960 to become America's first Roman Catholic president, John Kennedy cited the separation of church and state to comfort Protestants anxious that he might be subject to Rome instead of Washington. "I believe in an America where the separation of church and state is absolute, where no public official either requests or accept instructions on public policy from the Pope," he said on the second Monday of September, addressing the Greater Houston Ministerial Association. "I would not look with favour upon a president working to subvert the First Amendment's guarantees of religious liberty."

Kennedy embraced Roman Catholics, Protestants, and Jews, as America's religious pluralism always had. Only after the Holocaust, did we think embracing Jews required us to wind back Christianity.

My days and weeks working in Washington, late in 1998 and early '99, were too few. Mike was a bookish-looking lawyer with softly greying hairs and an unflappable calmness, while his mind worked through his considerable knowledge and expertise. A past managing partner of his law firm, he spoke proudly of the firm's efforts to inspire poor, black children to study and work.

Not just working with Mike, I enjoyed his and his family's hospitality. With many reasons I had to trust his judgement and not merely his character, Mike and I shared conversations over lunches and dinners, at his home and in restaurants. At least one was about the court and political actions to remove Christian prayer from American public schools.

Understanding it had been no coincidence, Mike told me the people so determined to separate church and state in America were Jews. (My Jewish friend Ian Biner was no less Mike's friend than I was, although his and my journeys never crossed in Washington.)

Once content for the countries in which they lived to be Christian, Jews had increasingly ceased tolerating Christianity since the Holocaust. So have we.

While other races continue presuming religion relates to all things, we separate church and state as an article of faith, even where there is no formal, legal separation. It's postmodern dogma, when we're so determinedly postmodern. Western states meld with multiculturalism, becoming defender of that faith.

No longer allowing Christians of all denominations into public office, separating church and state now prefers none of them. Upsetting Bob Hawke a decade earlier presumably wasn't the reason that in 2001, Prime Minister John Howard recommended the Queen appoint Anglican archbishop Peter Hollingworth to be governor-general. Australian Democrats leader Natasha Stott Despoja criticised the appointment as somehow breaching separation of church and state. It made no difference that Hollingworth would cease being archbishop before becoming governor-general, or that the latter was largely a ceremonial role.

Separating church and state now keeps Christians in check. Our multiculturalism would've loved appointing a rabbi or imam to be governor-general, but not a former archbishop. In 2007, Australian Democrats leader Lyn Allison complained there were too many Christians in parliament. No one says there are too many Muslims in government of a Muslim country.

While the West pursues peaceful coexistence between religions, we're not looking for one with Christianity. The West's solution to conflict between Christians of faith and the faithless is to demand tolerance from the faithful.

Greens senator Kerry Nettle thought Tony Abbott was ineligible to speak about a pill inducing abortions because he was Roman Catholic *"Mr Abbott,"* declared a tee shirt she wore, *"get your rosaries off my ovaries."* Other religions are at least equally concerned about abortions, but aren't so angrily dismissed from debate.

If separating church and state doesn't exclude the faithful from public office, we must leave our faiths behind. In 2011, a New South Wales politician sent a Christmas card laced with, of all things, Christianity. *"The idea of separation of church and state seems to have passed NSW Attorney-General Greg Smith by,"* lampooned the *Crikey* daily mail. In the West, Christmas and Christianity had passed.

A memorandum from America's House of Representatives franking commission the second Monday of December 2011 forbid taxpayer dollars funding Christmas cards. "I called the commission to ask for clarification and was told no 'Merry Christmas'," said a congressional staffer, affirming how close to complete the separation of God from government in America had become.

Other holidays don't fare any better. "Also told cannot say 'Happy New Year' but can say 'have a happy new year' – referencing the time period of a new year, but not the holiday." It's separation of holiday and state, but not calendar and state. Never was capitalisation of letters more important.

Any American government reach into schools had become a means to expel Christianity. Ellery Schempp was a Unitarian, who in 1956 believed Jewish students were upset to hear Bible readings in school. He thus upset Christians by bringing a Koran to school. (A Koran presumably did not upset Jews.) The result, with the help of the American Civil Liberties Union, was Schempp's court action against the Abington School District. The Supreme Court denied American children knowledge of the Bible in public schools: schools without education.

Not even Satan tried to ban Bible readings in heaven. He just left. The American Civil Liberties Union would've remained, and demanded God depart.

Since the Second World War, civil libertarians have set about denying Americans their liberties: their rights to religion, to congregate together, to a country. Time and again, they've led campaigns and court actions to ban prayer; the irony of being libertarians lost upon them. The liberties of people opposed to Christianity prevail over the liberties of American parents wanting their children to learn of their heritage in school and to practice their religion in public. Never before have the liberties of so few been wielded to deny liberties to so many.

It's the same through much of the West. In Australia, Toowoomba singer and jingle writer Ron Williams petitioned the High Court in 2011 to replace the National School Chaplaincy Programme with counsellors. Much like America, his argument was an interpretation of the Australian constitution the founding fathers never imagined: section 116 innocuously headed *"Commonwealth not to legislate in respect of religion."* Australia had long accorded Christian denominations equal (if separate) treatment, under a constitution with a preamble that spoke of the *"people...humbly relying on the blessing of Almighty God."* Nevertheless, Williams won most of his case.

"In a multicultural and multi-religious society," agreed New South Wales parliamentarian John Kaye, "the publicly funded chaplains are dangerous and unnecessary."

Kaye never explained what the dangers were. Critics don't complain vehemently about something merely for being unnecessary.

The decline of God's role guiding the West has been more than taken up by governments, corporations, organisations, and peoples without Him, quite apart from the media, films, and television. They're not, it seems, so dangerous. Nor are they unnecessary.

Multiculturalism means the onus is upon parents to teach their children the faiths of their forebears; we have no greater responsibilities to them. Parents of other races teach their children their faiths, but Western parents are busy. We've too much else to do to drop our children at Sunday school each week, as my parents-in-law dropped their children at a Methodist church while they did something else. (Addressing St Ives Baptist Church, school headmistress Megan Krimmer called it "the done thing" for parents in the 1960s and '70s.) They wouldn't have called themselves religious, but theirs was a time of religion.

Attending Presbyterian Church schools granted me hymns, chapel services, and divinity classes: my religious and other cultural heritage. After Knox Grammar School became part of the Uniting Church, it watered the divinity subject down to be religious education. Our teacher replaced the Bible with songs by American singer songwriter Jackson Browne.

At the time, I thought that was great. I was wrong, as children can be.

Freedom of religion or irreligious thought requires knowledge of our religion; people need to know something as much to reject it as believe it. Denying Western children a Christian education or other upbringing denies them their opportunity to choose what to think: their chances for faith. Uninformed choice is no choice at all. It's hard not to conclude that atheists denying children the knowledge to make up their minds lack the intellectual rigour to argue their atheism. Rather than win debates, they avert them.

Not just Christians of faith feel that way. As I learnt the day I attended a non-fiction writing class conducted by journalist Malcolm Knox, he'd attended the same school I did. He rebelled against his Protestant youth by becoming an atheist and never having a Protestant girlfriend. He married a Roman Catholic, in whose church their children were baptised. His fellow atheists criticised him for letting their children learn about God, but his reply explained why all children need religious education.

Children *"are too young to be atheists,"* he wrote in 2010, *"or for that matter believers. It is as an atheist that I wanted them to have religious education. It is as an atheist that I agree with Robert Forsyth, the Anglican Bishop of South Sydney, who says ethics classes should not be substitutes for scripture."*

Some of Knox's reasons apply to all children. Most apply only to Western children.

To paraphrase, Christian education gives children reason to wonder: to ask questions about life and the universe. It teaches them eternity. It's education about churches and other Christian features of our culture. Churches do good works helping poor people; "*caring for the underdog, distrusting materialism, cherishing the environment, and standing up against the corrupt*" are Christian precepts. Biblical stories are our children's birthright.

"*I don't see a church trying to indoctrinate, at least not in the old-fashioned way,*" wrote Knox. "*If the church is risking anything by dropping the hellfire, it's in not standing strongly for anything. That might not be the best thing for the church, but it is for my children.*" Besides, pretty much all the children's film, television, and literature he'd seen tried to indoctrinate children to particular political and social viewpoints. It normally failed.

Knox quoted film-maker Peter Weir to say the creative mind should escape endless activity, and take time to imagine and contemplate. "*A little boredom now and then, sitting in church while they're thinking about something else, can send them off to new places inside the lozenges of those stained-glass windows.*" They are places I, the adult, go too.

Oh, were it the case we're all willing to think, to explain our reasoning and understand our flaws? The music playing through prayers at our family Uniting church makes them more emotive than thoughtful.

Knox distinguished tolerance from indifference (as I like to do). Only people knowledgeable about religion can discuss it. Without knowledge, we're simply indifferent.

Multiculturalism depends upon ignorance of the cultures we're losing. We strip Christianity from the state and our schools, because it defies what we're trying to achieve: our new model earth.

12. ECONOMIC RELIGION

In an early nineteenth-century instance of unnatural selection, Hirschel Levi, a Jew, converted to Lutheran Christianity so he could continue working as a lawyer in the Rhineland after the Kingdom of Prussia took control, following Napoleon's defeat at Waterloo. He also changed his name to Heinrich Marx.

Like many others saying what his audience wants to hear to get what he wants, the conversion lacked conviction. His son Karl grew up in a home without religion, and became the primary figure in the development of communism.

Before discrimination for religious belief in employment became generally illegal and religion in Sydney became private, law firms were well known to be Protestant, Catholic, or Jewish. Freehill Hollingdale & Page was the largest Roman Catholic firm, Allen Allen & Hemsley the largest Protestant firm. Employers, aspiring employees (and clients) were free to discriminate. People preferred to work and deal with others of their religion.

Through the mid 1980s, I sat in law firm job interviews before Jew and Gentile alike, interested only in me. I never thought to mention religion. No interviewer did. All I called myself was a capitalist.

Businesses stopped allowing traditional religion ostensibly because we demand that employees respect each other's religions, although other people's religions were never so offensive when our countries were Christian as they became with multiculturalism. Suddenly, alluding to a person's religion offends someone of another religion, so none of us say anything.

We have more reasons than that to keep our faith to ourselves. We have our careers to consider.

Traditional religions contemplate something other than money motivating people to act, unlike our mass media advertisements. Religions offer joy from something other than shopping malls or holidays in expensive resorts. They speak of contentment (even salvation), without hunger to work and spend. Being religious can mean lacking ambition. We're not putting the company first.

From my experience, tradesmen of faith are most likely to perform quality work. When tiler Jono became more interested in cars than church, he became unreliable.

Superseding differences between religions requires superseding religions, unless another religion supersedes. There's never been a civilisation without something describable as religion, affording people purpose and comfort, satisfying our needs to believe in more than the mechanics of food, clothing, and shelter: something bigger than us. Addressing St Ives Baptist Church the first Sunday in October 2015, Pastor Guy said anthropologists have found all ancient peoples worshipped something.

"*If God did not exist*," observed French writer Voltaire in 1770, "*it would be necessary to invent him.*" Entrepreneurs like invention. The French Revolution rejected Christianity in favour of the Cult of Reason, while Maximilien Robespierre tried to install a new state religion: the Cult of the Supreme Being. Both failed, before being banned in 1802.

Even irreligious ideologies don't allow the vacuum of there being no religion. Soviet communists didn't lump their global, multicultural ideology with archaic notions of religion any more than we do, but theirs became an atheistic religion. After founder Vladimir Lenin died in 1924, the Soviet Union immortalised him with embalming fluids and kept his body on permanent display, allowing the faithful to continue homage. It was a little reminiscent of the Resurrection of Christ, but He spent only a short time on earth before rising to heaven. Since the Soviet Union was already heaven, its god lay in a Moscow mausoleum.

Not to be outdone, communist China did the same. (East Asians like to copy, although not multiculturalism.) Mao Zedong died in 1976, but still lies embalmed on public exhibition in Beijing. He was looking a little less than his prime when I saw him in 1988.

While many Russians since the collapse of communism have wanted Lenin buried, complex political and historical reasons mean he remains available for viewing. At least capitalists let people die.

Lenin and Mao can't compare with Kim Il-Sung, the founding dictator of the Democratic People's Republic of Korea (resulting from the Soviet Union liberating northern Korea from Japan at the end of World War II). Following his death in 1994, Kim Il-Sung lies in a mausoleum in Pyongyang, while the North Korean constitution recognises him as the *"eternal President of the Republic."* He remains the president for eternity.

It seems extraordinary to think of Christianity reaching into East Asian communism, but we had sent them our missionaries. With more than a passing similarity to the Biblical foretelling of Christ's birth almost two thousand years earlier, the official North Korean biography of Kim Il-Sung's son Kim Jong-Il claimed that a swallow foretold his birth at Mount Paektu, which a double rainbow over the mountain and a new star in the heavens heralded.

The Peoples Temple Agricultural Project at Jonestown, Guyana was a communist cult. In 1978, pumped up with Kool-Aid much as we now are with equality, more than nine hundred Americans committed suicide there in defence of socialism.

With the failure of multicultural communism, our multicultural vision needs something else to replace Christianity. Commerce is our first hope to supersede differences between religions, as it was between Christians and Jews. Our unfettered individualism created commercial religion, as we need it to do.

Without Christianity to keep us, capitalism (as much as communism) became a religion for atheists; it's all economics, political or not. A company is a legal entity potentially immortal (much like Kim Il-Sung). The omnipotent economy is Western God the Parent, whose child is each self-worshiping individual: mortal me. Ours is a holy duopoly, trying to mould us in its image. The Lord Western God is a jealous god.

The Christianity that empowered us to be free from other people's control, no longer does. Commercial hegemony is the things that we buy, paid for by what we sell, even if all we sell is our time at the office. What isn't production must be consumption. If we want to be happy, we buy something. In 2012, denim jeans were marketed under the brand name True Religion.

Employees and consumers adhere to a system of values: free market economics of supply and demand. Employers embrace those sharing their beliefs, whatever their physical or mental attributes. We find in our times our quests for success, without dwelling too much upon what success means: a job title and business expansion? Telling each other they're all that we need, we trust the company brochures. We don't want one Bible but expect a consumer-driven choice of management textbooks, often titled with a metaphor about animals. Faithless sceptics don't understand.

Western faith isn't in God. It's in human resources departments,

In December 2003, Cement Australia placed on each employee's desk a small plastic-wrapped packet, containing a silver-wrapped chocolate and four colourful postcards. Each card had a slogan and image unrelated to Christmas, but shining with summer. "*Recharge*," pictured two feet in flippers resting in an ocean reef. The holidays were time to recharge for another year working; that was all. Another card pictured a man without clothes looking up to blue sky, his arms stretched out Christ-like, foreshowing "*The future looks bright.*"

Marketing replaced the Messiah. This festival was based not upon the Son but the sun, with homage to our Christian past but without sense of a soul. Our places of work are our places of worship.

The company was the latest at which I worked to send cards around Christmas time wishing people "*Happy Holidays,*" or blander still "*Seasons Greetings*" and "*Festive Greetings.*" Not even that lasted. The two companies at which I worked thereafter didn't send anything, perhaps for the first being run by a Jew and the second an atheist.

We replaced the birth of one saviour with the periodic return of another. Santa Claus might've been inspired by the Christian bishop Saint Nicholas giving presents to good children, but he's long left Christianity to be patron saint of the post-Christian West.

The 2006 end-of-year pageant at our local primary school dutifully avoided reference to dissident religion, but featured an enthusiastic rendition of 'Jingle Bells' complete with the fat man in red coming on stage. Teachers and parents clapped. Children cheered. Boys and girls wearing red felt antlers, singing, and dancing kept the jolly fellow with them on stage. They kept him, and kept him.

Like green plastic trees and white polystyrene snow, he and his make-believe reindeers fill shopping centres throughout December, and through increasing numbers of weeks and months beforehand. The more children believe in Santa, whatever the faiths of their families, the greater the expectations imposed on mummy and daddy, auntie and uncle, grandma and grandpa.

Adults don't need to believe for the same expectations. Our

wide grins are the grins of getting new toasters and cappuccino machines; we've been good all year and deserve them. There are no judgements or morality, no offending anyone by deciding he or she has been bad, just presents.

No modern giver turns a lathe in a wood shop to make a new doll. Where there are presents, there's purchasing. The big S means more of the big S: sales.

So successful was the Coca Cola Company's marketing using Santa Claus' image, the myth arose that he donned red and white because they were Coca Cola's colours. The old boy wasn't about giving or children. He was about aerated cola.

There's thus great irony in some Christians of faith objecting to Santa as a distraction from the Biblical essence of Christmas. If people realised he was Christianity's last muttering at Christmas, then he would've been banned. By speaking to commerce, Santa survives.

The Hollings Cancer Centre in Charleston, part of the Medical University of South Carolina, was aware of the association between Santa and Christianity, even if retired insurance executive Frank Cloves wasn't. In November 2011, before irreligious Cloves' one day of the year coming to the centre dressed as Santa, it told him not to come. "Because of our state affiliation, we decided not to have a Santa presence this year," said Hollings spokeswoman Vicky Agnew. "People who are Muslim or Jewish or have no religious beliefs come here for treatment."

Instead, decorations would be "more secular and respectful to all beliefs," said Agnew. That meant wreaths, poinsettias, and garlands not respectful to anyone and so not disrespectful to anyone else. Less like a festival, they were more like a garden. Like our distant ancestors, we've become nature worshipers.

The director of the state chapter of the American Civil Liberties Union declined to comment. The union's website, with a high-minded tone far removed from any sense of festival, decreed "*some limited governmental celebrations of Christmas are not per se unconstitutional...the burden for the government to show that its activities do not have the purpose or effect of endorsing a religious message is high.*"

The American constitution wasn't originally so vacuous. It's hard to imagine Thomas Jefferson being so boring.

When a Christian connection is brought to our attention, we submit. Richard P was among my past colleagues from Holyman

Limited catching up before Christmas 2012. He said his brother played Santa at the Westfield Centre in Parramatta, but was forbidden from saying "Ho, Ho, Ho," for fear of provoking abuse and violence from Muslims. One Muslim Lebanese man took sight of Santa and assaulted him, before the Lebanese security guards escorted him away.

Our Jewish friend Ian Biner laughingly suggested that the security guards probably just told the Muslim to be quiet, saying: "There's not enough of us, yet."

Unperturbed about Muslim abuse and violence, our former colleague Liz set her sights upon Christians. She accused us of being hypocrites because the Book of Jeremiah forbids decorating trees, and so forbids Christmas trees.

I was surprised Liz, so devoutly an atheist, knew what the Book of Jeremiah said about anything, but there's nothing like a chance to criticise Christians for atheists to start citing the Bible and other atheists to recall every word. We don't quote the Torah or Koran to criticise Jews or Muslims; that would be intolerant. Besides, we've no idea what's in the Torah or Koran; they're not our religion. (We only know that they're both very reasonable.)

Not having a Bible with me at the time, I looked into Liz's claim later. The passage to which she referred has nothing to do with decorations. It forbids idolatry.

Within weeks after Christmas, come the first images of Easter. It's a rare child who can turn his mind on Good Friday to the Crucifixion of Christ, when steaming hot cross buns are brought out before him. The Easter morning Resurrection can seem very distant when there are sweet chocolate rabbits and eggs, all bought fresh from the bakery, supermarket, or dedicated chocolate shops. Consumers might diet. We never fast.

Western rule isn't by God, but by mammon. We don't need church when the stores are awash with religion to eat. God is irrelevant.

Even the Islamic period of fasting, we reduce to a matter of shopping. 'Ramadan shakes off retail gloom with a festive finish,' beamed a *Sydney Morning Herald* newspaper headline in 2011. The boom in sales was enough for the Bankstown Centro shopping centre to extend opening hours during Ramadan, with most of its three hundred and ten stores participating. (The 2006 census had found Muslims comprised fifteen percent of people in the

Bankstown council area.) The three-day celebration of *Eid al-Fitr*, the Festival of Breaking the Fast, was a time to spend money on clothes.

The reporter compiling the story, Leesha McKenny, wasn't the shopping reporter. She was responsible for religious affairs.

We'll see how atheistic religions fare. While the West finds God more offensive than materialism, I suspect many practicing Muslims and Jews take offence at the pervasiveness of commercialism. An immortal old man flying the world giving presents (provided he's not coming to the Hollings Cancer Centre in Charleston) is no less contrary to their views of the world than the Son of God born in a manger.

Abandoning God denied the West one resurrection but with everything commercial, we have commercial resurrection. No religion ever lied as freely as commercial advertising does.

After black American golfer Eldrick "Tiger" Woods was revealed late in 2009 to have carried out a series of sordid extramarital affairs with blonde women (as was his wife), some of his corporate sponsors abandoned him, but not the sporting goods manufacturer Nike. Restoring his image of the devoted family man, no matter how false it had proven to be, Nike's next television advertisement featured Woods standing solemnly before the camera. Addressing him was the voice of his father. "Tiger," said Earl Woods, "I am prone to be inquisitive, to promote discussion. I want to find out what your thinking was. I want to find out what your feelings are, and did you learn anything?"

The advertisement didn't mention Earl having been an adulterer too. Nor did it mention he'd been dead for almost four years.

A day or more would elapse before someone revealed the words weren't even directed to his son. A recording of an interview Earl Woods gave had been edited to make it sound as if they were. "Authoritarian," he said, back in 2004, responding to a question about his Thai wife, Kultida. (Celebrating diversity could've had a field day with that family, without mentioning adultery.) "Yea, Tida is very authoritative. She is very definitive: 'Yes' and 'No.' I am more prone to be inquisitive, to promote discussion. I want to find out what your thinking was, I want to find out what your feelings are and did you learn anything?"

If executives decide Tiger Woods' father isn't the only person enjoying life after death, companies will advertise inside coffins and crematorium chambers. Others will charge tolls for the journeys to heaven and hell.

13. RELIGION FOR SALE

The children at our local primary school recite the school pledge at each weekly assembly. The boys of my sons' scout troops recite the scout pledge at every meeting. "I honour my god," they begin, as they must if every child in a religiously plural group is to speak truthfully. Reducing all religions to equivalence, they're words for non-believers, without sense of any true God. Treating religions equally makes none of them real. There's no deep belief (like the Baha'i).

When America began printing her motto on coins from 1864 and the rest of her currency from 1956, there was conviction. "*In God we trust*," they say, not "*In my God we trust.*"

Christianity commands the truth, but in our increasing desire since the Second World War to avert religious conflict and with the problem of religions being contradictory, we've stopped believing in facts. (We still have conflicts with recalcitrant Christians, but we have all sorts of problems with them.) The West rejects reality, when reality could cause offence.

Relativism means we each have our own truths, each religion its own. There are none about God, or very much else.

Our children's primary school pledge goes on, "I am loyal to my school. I respect my flag." The only loyalty the children afford is to school, which doesn't make the school great. It makes God and the flag small. With children from so many countries, what was "our flag" became merely "my flag."

Every time we think globally, we're each of us alone, not just on earth but throughout the universe. The only person to serve is me.

Canadian Girl Guides did away with their oath to God and the Queen in favour of one to "to be true to myself, my beliefs, and Canada." It's hardly an oath but a statement a girl will please herself and, provided she's not inconvenienced, be true to Canada. Murderers, rapists, and paedophiles think they're true to themselves.

Conviction depends upon confidence there are facts to know. Mere beliefs lack conviction.

Since 2012, New South Wales Girl Guides needn't even be true to their beliefs. They merely "develop my beliefs." They should have no conviction, but be forever working towards it.

As well as removing God and the Queen from the pledge, commissioner Belinda Allen objected to the sixth Guide law: "A Guide is obedient." She preferred the word so commonplace in our self-determined values: "respect."

Whatever respect means, it doesn't mean obedience. It never did. A guide can do whatever she likes, trying not to upset anyone else; well, almost anyone.

What remains are personal beliefs about God and godlessness: transient arrays of whatever abstractions each person wants, for as long as he or she wants them. Western multiculturalism makes religion fickle, coming as it does without the authority of a nation or people but only a number of private opinions.

Our failure to provide religious conviction doesn't just leave people with little reason to believe our religion. It leaves them vulnerable to everything else. In his 1775 speech on conciliation with America, Irish rationalist Edmund Burke said "religion, and not atheism, is the true remedy of superstition."

If the postmodern West believes anything aside from our economies and ideologies, it's typically an undefined, uncertain, personal plaything we call spirituality. It can be no more than a means of politely respecting all religions without believing any. Everyone should be pleased and no one offended. Conversation can move quickly onto property prices.

Calling Scientology a church rather than a business aids recruitment. It also offers tax exemption.

Spirituality comes without morals telling people what to do. If it did, people wouldn't select it. It comes without conscience or command, except as a reason to do whatever someone would've done anyway. (Biblical preaching is much too prescriptive.) Western people want spirituality to help them feel good, legitimising themselves in their lifestyles and lives. Anything else, they refuse.

Englishman C.S. Lewis refined his reasons to believe Christianity to their essence in his book *Mere Christianity*. The West has mere spirituality: anything ephemeral outside the physical and immediately practical. It might be interest in personality, character, or values. It could even, God help us, be this book.

Mere spirituality can be religion for display: an ornamental motif. Crystal quartz and polished gemstones stand on living room mantelpieces, no more noticed than a vase or porcelain figure. The crystal could calm, people said, much like I imagine computer screens of tropical aquariums. At a whim, inside a small shop in Glebe with my friend Megan among others in 1992, I bought a small crystal. My interest in geology had been dormant too long.

For all its geological detail, it's a rock, no more calming than a vase or figurine and much less calming than pixels of fish. My crystal soon lay in a box, among the vestiges of my teenage stone collection.

"People no longer believing in God don't believe in nothing," says an old adage attributed to English writer G.K. Chesterton, "but in everything." That is, with the right marketing.

In response to me asking what she did, at a party held by a fellow parishioner Graham at St Anne's Church in Ryde, a woman with powder-white skin and jet-black long hair described herself as a "white witch." She spoke as another person might call herself a real estate agent, except that she refused to explain what being a white witch meant, particularly to people calling ourselves Christians. It would presumably be like having to explain what a real estate agent was. Perhaps she charged money to reply, wanting three eyes of newt. Perhaps she simply sold real estate.

Travel agents offering return trips to nirvana are still travel agents. Nirvana for me would be Scrumpy Jack cider in an old English village. Drinking a couple of pints, I'm very spiritual.

Spirituality for sale is more of a transaction than dropping anonymous money into an offertory plate. It's at least as valid an amenity as electronic can openers or the pleasure of a stone flamingo on the balcony. Customers aren't buying truth but belief, equating perception to fact. They can believe they control the universe or believe nobody does; whatever they want. Without any more questioning than the rest of our consumption, they feel what they want to feel. Hope, meaning, and destiny become self-fulfilling promises.

All the trappings of Christianity we can find in our spiritual free markets: free market prophecy, free market communion. People speak of beliefs as if they've always believed them, but with each new belief they forget what they previously believed. Books, ornaments, and courses about ancient Viking runes provided the older of my sisters with the universe she wanted, until she found her next universe to buy.

At least runes are European. My sister is not Scandinavian.

Sweden's official recognition of Norse paganism as a religious community (allowing it to apply for government funding and marry couples) wasn't a matter of honouring her cultural heritage, any more than was the same recognition granted to elves and gnomes. If it were, then at the end of 2011 she wouldn't have recognised Isak Gerson's Church of Kopimism. Its three thousand members met weekly to share computer files containing music, films, and other content they considered holy. Copying them was sacrament.

Never was our smorgasbord of nonsensical religions more commercial, and our cultureless West more obviously political economics. Purgatory was presumably a computer crashing. Hell was being unable to retrieve the files.

The more ridiculous the belief, the ruder it becomes for the rest of us to challenge it. Western multiculturalism commands that we treat religions equally, no matter how stupid they are.

There's no greater misnomer than claiming ours is an age of science. For all our assertions of science, we choose not to pose questions about water divining or extrasensory perception. We'd believe someone claiming to be psychic when he quotes communications with a hundred-year-old tortoise. We'd accept his word the tortoise told him it was missing a blanket somebody in the audience knitted. Ours is an age without science.

Wherever there's a product or service for sale, there are sellers earning money. Spirituality for sale must entertain, much like performing monkeys on a music box for which passers-by drop coins in a hat. Astrologers offering good times to come are never more than a phone call away, charging by the half minute.

Christianity at an Australian Corporate Lawyers' Association Christmas party would've been unethical and insensitive to people of other religions and of no religion at all, but for several years a sponsor (the Mahlab legal recruitment firm) hired two colourfully robed tarot card readers to perform there. The soothsayers sat at low tables, before which stood queues of corporate lawyers in our fully breasted suits. No lawyers admitted to me they believed what they'd been told, but many let their eyes drift from our conversation unwilling to dismiss out of hand their futures foretold. After all, their fortunes were good.

I don't like joining queues, but the queue the last day of November 2007, at the Georges Mediterranean bar and restaurant by Darling Harbour, sat on lounges with glasses of wine. That was my kind of queue. My glass in hand, I joined the game. Finally I sat before a woman in flowing black and purple cloth, calling herself a psychological astrologer. Perhaps the psychologist in her title meant she thought about astrology, instead of just copying the magazine charts. It might've meant she charged our sponsor more.

She asked me the date and time I was born. I told her, as best as I knew the time. As she asked me to do, I shuffled piles of tarot cards, face down, and broke them into more piles. I chose one pile, which she took. She turned a card over and laid it face up before me, and then another. She continued flicking them onto a spreading pile of cards, sometimes pausing at one. "You have great challenges," she told me.

"No."

"What I meant," she explained, "was confusion."

"No," I said, before helping her along. "I have uncertainty."

"Yes!" she exclaimed. "That's what I meant."

She made several wrong suggestions. We discussed each of them, until she explained that what I told her was what she'd really meant from the beginning.

Nevertheless, she said something worthwhile. She referred me to an inscription in the Temple of Apollo at Delphi, although I didn't recall seeing it when I visited the ruined temple in 1993. (I learnt later that the Greek traveller Pausanias in the second century after Christ described it in the forecourt.) *"Know Thyself."*

She probably meant us individuals. She should've meant the West by this time in our history, such as it is.

She encouraged me to write, as she seemed to encourage everyone to work. It was advice corporate lawyers expected to hear and act upon without difficulty. I took her business card. (If Jesus Christ returns today to the West, He'd better have a business card.)

Mere spirituality for professional people is normally a little self-centric meditation, led by a paid consultant. The Australian Corporate Lawyers' Association convened complimentary meditation sessions, conducted by a former corporate lawyer with whom I'd attended law school, Sandy. (I had to tell my secretary

Katrina that the word *"meditation"* wasn't a misprint for *"mediation."*) The meditation among two dozen or so lawyers was a pleasant time sitting down, fun even. Subsequent sessions would've cost money.

Decorating our local railway station soon afterwards was a poster advertising college classes in meditation. The poster pictured a business analyst sitting in a field with his eyes closed, legs crossed, and fingers clasping the Lotus position (derived from Hinduism and Buddhism). Meditation, said the caption, helped him clarify his plans to open a coffee shop.

Christian meditation dwells upon God. The meditation the West prefers is spiritual individualism, focusing already self-absorbed minds even more on their individual selves and careers.

Claiming spirituality while eschewing theistic religion doesn't take people closer to God than we get by contemplating our navels, but God isn't where the West is trying to go. (At least contemplating other people's navels can take people part way towards God, in the right circumstances.) Each spiritual loner sits alone amidst a revolving universe, believing whatever he or she bought to believe.

Western gullibility was never more bizarre than in the trepidation people gave the twenty-first day of December 2012, because the Mayan calendar ended that day. People presumed the Mayans thus knew the date the world would end. The 2009 American film *2012* was the most obvious profiteering from it all. (Immersed as the West is in the notion of truth being subjective, films and television programmes are as real as anything else persuading us what to love and what else to dread.)

When the apocalypse didn't occur that morning, people weren't perturbed. Someone came up with eleven minutes past ten o'clock that evening, Sydney time, as the more precise moment. We had more hours to fret. More than thirty schools in Michigan closed early that day, in part because of the prediction. Matt Wandrie, superintendent for Lapeer Community Schools, said doomsday "rumours" were rampant in several districts.

The Mayan calendar meant nothing more than does any other calendar. The annual Law Society diary didn't mean lawyers forecast the world ending on the last day of December each year.

Mayans had never suggested the world was going to end that day in 2012. The idea came from the West. Western demands for something in which to believe gave great credence to nonsense.

We'd done a lot of that since losing Christian conviction.

Someone said it was all an excuse for a party. In our nihilistic individualism, we worry about everything and care about nothing.

The contrast between religious lives and lives without is never more striking than in the moments of our passing. The second Friday of February 2013, my wife and I attended separate funerals a hundred miles apart. Both deceased were more than ninety years of age, but my wife's Aunt Dulcie wasn't a woman of faith. Nor were her closest relatives, none of whom spoke at the service. A marriage celebrant conducted the service in a funeral chapel, with the same shallow words she surely spoke for every stranger's passing: Dulcie would live forever in their hearts.

It was all very facile. The service was over after twenty-five minutes, with my wife wanting to cry out, "There must be something more!"

Reverend Roy's funeral lasted more than two hours, accommodating three hundred and ninety-five mourners. His family, priests, and the Returned Services League spoke their thoughts, expressed as much through words of the Bible as the trumpet sounding the Last Post. Loved as he was, nobody said Roy lived forever in their hearts. He had eternal life.

Little wonder that families without religious faith are dispensing with funerals altogether. There were no funerals for my wife's Uncles Lloyd and Harold, although the family shared a nice lunch when they knew Harold's death was soon coming.

As the French writer Voltaire lay on his deathbed, a priest asked him to turn back to God and renounce the Devil. "Sirs," Voltaire reputedly replied, "this is no time to be making new enemies."

The West readying for our deathbed has much the same approach. Voltaire at least believed there was a god.

14. SPORT

Ancient Greeks performed amateur games at Mount Olympus. Happiness was real.

Sports like cricket were part of English culture, not just to play and watch but to think much about. We played with passion and honour, but participation, attendances, and television ratings all plummeted as other cultures took hold. So did the honour. Hostile to everything English, my friend Peter, formerly the finance manager at Holyman Limited, thought cricket was boring.

Living in the Sutherland Shire, Peter often said only three things in life were important: "the Shire, the Saints, and the Sharks." The Saints and Sharks were the St George and Cronulla rugby league teams.

In his 1843 manuscript *Contribution to the Critique of Hegel's Philosophy of Right*, revolutionary Karl Marx famously described religion as the *"opium of the people,"* comforting the exploited and impoverished peasantry, thereby deterring it from revolution. *"Religious distress is at the same time the expression of real distress and the protest against real distress,"* he wrote, in a style as easy to follow as that of any modern management consultant or political apologist. *"Religion is the sigh of the oppressed creature, the heart of a heartless world, just as it is the spirit of a spiritless situation... The abolition of religion as the illusory happiness of the people is required for their real happiness. The demand to give up the illusion about its condition is the demand to give up a condition which needs illusions."*

Spectator sport is the opium of our postmodern West. Fans scream for a wicket, moan for a miss. We rant for victory and weep for a loss; football and hockey hooligans riot as much for one as the other. Again human in all our emotions, we repeat joy and vitriol when next our team plays, quick to vent both.

As if they were museum artefacts or church relics, sporting memorabilia decorated the offices of Horsell insurance brokers in Sydney 2006, financed by the principals' private superannuation fund. Not just the signed football jerseys that grace many bars, they included a cricket bat used by Don Bradman.

Sportsmen are postmodern gladiators: Davids against Goliaths, William Tells, Robin Hoods. There's bravery and heroism, if only for a ball. Fans feel a little like heroes each time their heroes fight: battles for people spared fighting real wars. Sports are the wars in which nobody dies.

"It's the only thing that keeps me going," said my friend Peter, the first Friday of January 2008, while working for a company providing banking services (without being a bank). He presumably wasn't thinking about cricket.

For my part, I'd liked being employed through Melbourne Cup day, when Babcock & Brown celebrated the horse race with a cocktail party, sweepstakes, and Calcutta. (Only fund management companies and the like could concoct a Calcutta: a costly combination of sweepstake and auction between syndicates trying to nab the eventual race winner.) Evoking his Roman Catholic heritage and the days canon law expected Roman Catholics to attend Mass, Peter described Melbourne Cup day as "one of the Days of Obligation."

Sport allows acutely private people to discuss (even debate) something other than work, food, and wine, without risking relationships being formed in a workplace any more than a stadium. The human resources general manager at Cement Australia rarely allowed conversations to venture beyond vocation, but spoke passionately about rugby union.

Rugby union is the sport of our commercial elite; Marx viewed everything in terms of class structure. The French investment bank for Otter Gold Mines Limited didn't employ a former Australian Wallabies captain (previously a College of Law student with me) for his legal or banking skills. A decade later, Nick was a director. "There wasn't a chief executive of a major French company who wouldn't cancel any appointment for a chance to talk with him about rugby," explained a bank executive at a lavish ball in the Sydney Town Hall. He might've spoken of major English, Australian, New Zealand, and South African companies too.

Sport and Christianity can coexist. Nick waived his usual speaking fees to address a dinner at our family Uniting church in the winter of 2015, as he waived them to address any church.

Before I'd joined Otter, the French bank flew its chief financial officer to Banff for a skiing holiday, for which Otter's chief executive never stopped complaining. (Pat complained about many things.) I'd have also accepted the bank's invitation, and I can't ski.

Never did TNT Limited seem more tribal than the early evenings when a dozen employees donned our company tee shirts to play touch football against teams representing other employers. A decade later, the former group legal counsel Frank jogged through the streets of North Sydney, wearing his white tee shirt with the long-obsolete company logo.

Employment has become too fickle to sustain company tribalism. Professional teams are more enduring. Blazing from a cap and flag I bought when a Finnish lawyer took my wife, baby son, and me to an ice hockey game in 1996 are the Helsinki I.F.K. red and white. Any beloved team can be a poor man's identity.

For Australian rugby league fans, it can also be their funeral rites. Coffins can be painted with the team colours and logo, presumably including those of the team's corporate sponsors.

Sports are more market economics, and not just for the television subscriptions and jerseys emblazoned with sponsors' logos. We barrack for teams owned by rich magnates as if our membership dues or season ticket makes the team ours. Fans of Formula One car racing wave flags of major motoring companies much richer than they'll ever be.

Consumers buy the best value and discard the rest. Success is part of the purchase. Australian interest in round ball football depends on the national team winning. Sydney's interest in Australian football depends on the Sydney Swans winning. (Writing this, I pause to check scores.) Codes offer the masses a plethora of teams, where a fan is loyal if he recalls the name of the team he backed when it won. Our loyalty is often no more than applause, from good-weather admirers who boo their team losing.

In Gettysburg, Pennsylvania, one Friday night in 1998, I wandered alone into a bar and befriended some young men from Ohio. Unlike most people who talk about sport, they also played it; they were still young enough to do so. They'd come to Gettysburg not for the Civil War history that brought me there, but to play football. When I mentioned my infant son with the middle name Cleveland, one of them insisted he have a Cleveland Indians baseball cap. Taking my work address because I never disclosed my home address, he duly sent a cap to him.

Ours is sport without exercise. Sports fans need no more play sport than we need to manufacture a dishwasher to clean dishes, unless our business is playing sport or manufacturing dishwashers. People who play sport normally talk a little less about it, unless they're being paid to do so.

Sportspeople become model heroes and heroines for what we think people should be (another ploy of our politics), especially when they're from other races. One television joker observed that our Western cultural elite who normally dismiss sport for being uncouth watch the football (soccer) World Cup because it's multiracial.

In 1998, New York ferry service manager Tom and his family shared Thanksgiving Day lunch with me in their New Jersey home. My keepsake was a *Sports Illustrated* magazine edition with a hologram image of Michael Jordan on the cover. If people knew only one basketball player, we knew Michael Jordan.

Sportspeople are what employers think employees should be. Australian cricketing characters with paunch bellies and smiles in their games, gave way to cold-hearted professionals who sledge their opponents.

Addressing a Cement Australia senior leadership conference I attended (and a sales and marketing division conference I didn't) in 2006, former Wallabies captain John Eales spoke of the need, above everything else, for a total commitment to winning. For us to bask in his presence, the cost-conscious company paid him twenty thousand dollars.

If a man's business is playing, then for more money or a better chance at winning a championship, he'll transfer from one team to another, one country to another. A professional sportswoman can represent one country and live where she likes. Fans cheer and abuse players who, like us, take the best jobs they can get.

"We should be like a football team," said my Jewish friend Ian Biner of Holyman Limited, at which he was business development manager, "where the only important thing is the team." France won the 1998 World Cup, not a son of Algerian immigrants Zidane Zidane or anyone else on the team. France, not the Algerians' son, butted Italian player Marco Materazzi's head eight years later. Only the jersey (with the team sponsor's logo) and the role in the team are important: forward, full back, goalkeeper.

It's our post-racial vision. We see the colours of jerseys, but not of the players. Physical features endure only when performance related.

Sport is a rare situation in which nations still mean anything in the West. More than merely a word on a form, we accept, encourage, and even expect sporting loyalty to our citizenry as we don't tolerate nationalism otherwise; we cheer together with people who, a day later, we'd let die in the street. Countries become tribal, with national selection warranting what race and religion no longer do. An American whose kin come forever from Ireland will support an American Pakistani sportsman playing an Irishman, with all thoughts of nation but none about race. Tiny tiers of loyalty they may be, but any short loyalty is better than none.

I think it was back in the 1990s, a tennis player complained that Australian crowds were notorious for supporting local players and not clapping others. For that, I recall, a commentator called Australian crowds ugly. When no Australians remained in the Australian Open one year, crowds barracked for an American whose father was Australian.

For all our supposed sports nationalism, crowds at the 2000 Olympic Games in Sydney cheered talented competitors and characters who tried, whatever their countries. We cheered every runner coming home in the marathons, making a hero or heroine of each who reached the stadium and finished.

Like other vestiges of human identity, marketers tap into patriotism if it helps sell their sports. Kangaroos fight and lions roar whenever promoting matches between Australia and England. Cricketers talk of an "old enemy" and a nineteenth-century urn of ashes.

When patriotism risks profit, it's discarded. A rugby union game I attended never mentioned the Waratahs having been New South Wales and the Hurricanes having been Otago; pay television subscribers from all over the world watch games feeling involved in the outcome. (More accurately, the Waratahs were the H.S.B.C. Waratahs. The Hong Kong and Shanghai Bank changed its name to H.S.B.C. in 1998 for much the same reason.) Mentioning geographical origin would be like mentioning head office on a bottle of soft drink.

I was a guest of the Willis insurance brokers. Sport is never better to watch than through corporate hospitality.

Races other than ours aren't as superficial as we've become. Chinese people supported Chinese American tennis player Michael

Chang for being Chinese. (Without thought about race, a few faithful Christian Australians I knew liked Chang because he mentioned God after a match.)

Thai people supported Tiger Woods for being a quarter Thai, but no internationally famous golfers were half Thai or Thai. (Golf courses are such beautiful places, striking a ball across green turf to a hole ruins a nice walk.) Thais wouldn't have been so supportive had Woods competed against someone more Thai.

Sport doesn't build the belonging between races and religions the West imagines it does. A few London black cab drivers (the cabs were black, not the drivers) told me they'd lost interest in English cricket when Africans and Asians entered the team.

Representing the Young Australian soccer team at the Asian championships for players less than nineteen years of age in 2010, Kerem Bulut won the Golden Boot for scoring seven goals. He was also a member of the Muslim Brotherhood Militants, and was among five teenagers who'd commenced a violent crime spree two months earlier. He faced Burwood Local Court charged with two counts of robbery in company, one count of participating in a criminal group to assist criminal activity, and two counts of threatening a person to influence a witness (all unrelated to the Young Australian soccer team).

Australia's male weightlifting team needed to finish among the top five at the Oceania Championships in Samoa to send a lifter to the 2012 Olympic Games in London. Seeing his opportunity, Daniel Koum threatened to withdraw if his teammates didn't pay him five thousand dollars. Team coach Michael Keelan said later he thought "it was a despicable act and I still feel that way," but felt the team's interest required him to arrange payment.

"I think it would be unprecedented in Australian sporting history," said sports lawyer Tim Fuller.

They spoke without thought about race. Koum was born in Cameroon.

Tempting then it is to complete the passage by Marx. Real happiness requires the abolition of professional sport, sports marketing, and their illusion of happiness. Only then will the West demand change to our conditions that need illusion.

15. OTHER PEOPLE'S FESTIVALS

Many a culture has festivals and feast days, often fun and meaningful, with traditions a people treasure. We treasure them too. Each year since 2010, the historical city of Parramatta has briefly become Parramasala for a festival of South Asian arts and cultures. In his last weeks of school, my eldest son's high school hosted a Moon Festival of Chinese and Korean performances, traditional games, and information stalls.

Religious events are a chance to bring different cultures together, according to Alex Kubienski, vice captain at Punchbowl Boys High School in 2012. He joined the Muslim majority of students by fasting through Ramadan. Principal Jihad Dib hosted Ramadan dinners for all staff and students. A member of the Jewish Board of Deputies, Melissa McCurdie from St Ives, also attended.

Christian festivals apparently aren't such a chance. Most of our festivals involved Christianity, even if they took our previous pagan religions into account. When we link our culture to religion, we don't accept our religion. We reject our culture.

Multiculturalism makes our religion offensive, as other religions aren't. The Montessori Marvels Preschool in Greenvale, Victoria replaced its 2010 Christmas party with an end-of-year party supposedly to be inclusive of all cultural groups (thereby inclusive of none). Children parted for the holidays wishing each other "Happy New Year." Calendars aren't as offensive as Christmas.

Spokeswoman Marlene Guclu was a Christian of faith, but that was her private matter. "We are just trying to take an open approach to the holiday season," she said. "We run a non-denominational, non-religious programme." The carols they sang changed the words to remove any hint of religion, although teachers could still mention Christmas in private conversations with individual children. "We want all families to feel welcome, of all nationalities."

Ethnic Communities Council of Victoria chairman Sam Afra wanted more preschools to do the same. "I would like to encourage more debate," he said, "and to be more mature about our debate, where we are more understanding and respect each other."

There'd been no debate and is no debate. We think debate would be insensitive to people of other races.

In our determination to welcome them, we'll experience their cultures but not risk them feeling uncomfortable about being exposed to ours. We've given up the beliefs and behaviours, rituals and customs that distinguished us from other races, forfeiting our festivals and fun because they were ours.

We consider asserting our culture to be mean. At Christmas time 2013, my second daughter said suggesting Christmas is more important than Hanukkah wasn't very nice. "Of course, it is," I told her. "I'd expect a Jew to say Hanukkah is more important than Christmas. I'd expect a Muslim to say Ramadan is more important."

Regulations under the Education and Care Services National Acts, passed in 2011 by Australian state and territory governments, provided that children in childcare centres not be *"required to undertake activities that are inappropriate, having regard to each family's family and cultural values..."* (That didn't extend to a whole raft of traditional Western family and cultural values at odds with multiculturalism.)

"As is already the case in government schools," said childcare minister Kate Ellis, "they are...focused on making sure that children are not made to feel uncomfortable because they are forced to participate in cultural traditions that are not their own."

Specifically mentioned was religion. "If you have a centre with a high Muslim population," said Early Childhood Australia chief Pam Cahir, "you're not going to be asking them to decorate a Christmas tree. I think common sense should prevail."

In practice, we're dispensing with Western culture altogether. We don't need a high Muslim population to end Christmas and Easter, but just one child who's not Western or is Western whose parents object. My wife told me the preschool our children attended wrote a note to all parents in 2006 saying that if any of them felt offended by Christmas, then the preschool wouldn't celebrate it. The parent needn't give a reason. It wasn't a matter of a majority of parents being offended, or even a sizeable minority. There needed be only one.

We're not just keeping that child from our culture. We're keeping our children too. While participation in events promoting multiculturalism (such as the multicultural speaking competitions at our local primary school) is compulsory, we forbid participation in events that are actually cultural, when the culture is ours.

My eldest son's year-five teacher banned the children in her class from giving each other Christmas cards with little red and white-striped candy canes. "It's not Elisha's religion," explained Mrs Smith, referring to a Muslim girl from Malaysia. (The child could just as easily have been a Buddhist boy from Nepal or a frog worshipper from the swamp.) Mrs Smith might have never asked Elisha what she thought. Our presumption other races find our cultures offensive doesn't depend on them feeling offence. We just fear that they might.

What remains of our culture is Christian in name only. Even that's proving too much.

For a while there, our children's primary school convened an Easter Hat Parade, without any further reference to Easter. Christ's death and Resurrection gave way to headwear. In 2008, the parade ended its last connection, however slight, to Christianity by becoming the Hilarious Head Hullaballoo, and not merely to include children who didn't wear hats. (The fifth school newsletter that first term misspelt "*hilarious*" as "*hillarious*." Multiculturalism matters more than spelling.)

Holidays remain times to talk of religion, but not ours. My youngest son's year-four class began 2012 Holy Week not with a story about Jesus dying on the Cross, but an Aboriginal story about two Googarh orphan goannas (whose mother had been killed by hunters) and a carpet snake. That Good Friday, my son repeated the story more thoroughly than most children could describe the Crucifixion.

My second son later recalled his year-two class marking the end of 2009 by celebrating religion, but not Christianity. The class performed Indian dances, with Hindu red dots on their foreheads. Christians uncomfortable about being required to participate would be spoilsports for saying so.

The 2010 concert carefully avoided all hint of Christmas, bar one: 'Jingle Bells'. Carols had long gone. There was no babe in a manger. One other moment I thought Christmas might get a look-in was when a few children entered the stage wearing sheets, because I assumed they were shepherds. They weren't. They were ghosts.

Apparently ghosts don't offend anyone. The class went onto perform the theme song from the film *Ghostbusters*.

The only reference to Christianity was in a roundabout way: the letter C. My youngest son's class danced to the old Village People song 'Y.M.C.A.' Long before they performed that little number, Y.M.C.A. was an abbreviation for the Young Men's Christian Association, although it's hard to imagine any group of men more antithetical to the original values of that association than the Village People. Our children's primary schoolteachers wouldn't have worried about the Village People's homosexuality, but may well have had tizzies if someone realised the C referred to something being Christian. They could've changed the C to, for example, an H.

After thirty-nine years of nativity plays and carol singing, Albert Park Preschool abolished Christmas in 2011. The only decoration was a tree made of tinsel decorated with children's handprints. An end-of-year concert comprised what journalist Susie O'Brien called "*non-carol Christmas songs*," such as 'Jingle Bells' and 'Santa Claus is Coming to Town'. The last newsletter to parents that year wished them a "*happy holiday season*" and a "*count down towards holidays and a variety of celebrations.*"

We don't have festivals. We have holidays, without sense that holidays abbreviated holy days. With nothing left in our lives but our commerce, all we comprehend are workdays, weekends, and holidays.

Our new teaching framework required preschools to "show respect for diversity," explained teacher Melissa Popley. "I believe," she said, sounding very religious, "and I have had to convert others about this – that to focus on just one religion is not inclusive of our kinder community."

We focus on none. Whatever her kinder community is, Christianity isn't part of it.

Demands for inclusion don't end with religion. I half expect to hear 'Rudolph the Red Nosed Reindeer' and 'I Saw Momma Kissing Santa Claus' become 'Rudolph the Special Needs Sleigh Puller' and 'I Saw My Primary Caregiver Kissing Santa Claus'.

"Funny thing about Christmas tree lights, actually," said a character in the 2008 Australian film *The Square*, "you know they're mostly manufactured in countries where they don't actually celebrate Christmas." I thought at first he was referring to Australia, America, or any number of other Western countries, but he was referring to China and other Asian countries.

We in the West no longer waste our productive labour manufacturing things. We expend it on court cases about Christmas.

The Catholic League won a legal challenge allowing a nativity scene in Penn Station, New York, where a menorah was already displayed in recognition of Hanukkah. In 2010, the New York Department of Transportation evicted a nativity scene from the St George Ferry Terminal, Staten Island but allowed a Christmas tree, along with a menorah. Legal precedent had considered them not religious symbols but, in the words of spokesman Seth Solomonow, "holiday symbols."

A nativity scene survived at Borough Hall, New York, beside a menorah, Christmas tree, and display for Kwanzaa (an African American celebration of traditional African values). White Americans rush about each December not to say "Merry Christmas," but "Happy Kwanzaa."

In November 2010, the Chase Bank told local businessman Antonio Morales to remove a Christmas tree he'd donated to its branch in Southlake, Texas. It wasn't a nativity scene representing baby Jesus in the manger or other representation of Christ's birth. It wasn't a representation of Christ. It was simply a tree. "Unfortunately," said bank spokesman Greg Hassell, although I'm not sure he meant it, "we're unable to keep it on display for the remainder of the holiday season." The only decorations were to be "something everyone is comfortable with, regardless of how they celebrate the season." That meant stickers resembling lights.

Hassell rejected the suggestion that the bank opposed Christmas. "People wish their customers Merry Christmas when it's appropriate." By that, he can't have meant when anyone could hear.

Great drama erupted in the town of Perkins, Oklahoma in December 2010 when Federal Reserve examiners from Kansas City arrived to inspect the Payne County Bank, as they did every four years. No money was missing, no customers or employees were aggrieved, but the examiners found something much worse. On the teller's counter were Crosses, a Bible verse of the day, and buttons saying *"Merry Christmas, God With Us."*

The Federal Reserve ordered their removal (or the matter would be referred to the Department of Justice to enforce), because they breached regulation B of the Bank Regulations pursuant to the Equal Credit Opportunity Act, prohibiting *"the use of words, symbols, models and other forms of communication which express, imply, or suggest a discriminatory preference or policy of exclusion."* The examiners feared a Jew, Muslim, or atheist could feel discriminated against by the bank.

The problem in Perkins wasn't actual discrimination but the appearance of possible discrimination, to a person who mightn't ever enter the bank. We're ending our culture, because maintaining it could seem discriminatory.

"They are taking Christ out of Christmas and life," complained Chelsi Holser, a bank customer.

The revolt by customers led to senator Jim Inhofe and congressman Frank Lucas issuing a joint letter to Federal Reserve chairman Ben Bernanke. "This is an all-out assault on the faith, values, and rights of the bank, its employees, and the people of Perkins they serve," said Inhofe. "It…unduly discriminates against a person's faith in Christ and their constitutionally protected freedom to publicly express that faith."

The West no longer understands religion, but understands politics. The second in command at the Federal Reserve promptly contacted the bank, letting it restore its Christian signs and symbols.

Without such acts of resistance, Western multiculturalism subsumes Western Christianity. When we're not adopting the traditions and rituals of other races, we're regressing to pagan times. Like our ancient ancestors, we worship the seasons: summer, autumn (or fall), winter, and spring. If we don't imagine sharing it with other races, then at least we know they won't be upset.

Christmas becomes the nondescript Summer or Winter Holiday, with capital letters. The lack of Christ in the word lets reference to Easter endure a little bit longer, although a week before Easter 2010, the city of Davenport, Iowa cited the city's religious diversity to rename Good Friday as the Spring Holiday. The uproar that led to the decision being hurriedly reversed will become less likely to succeed with each passing year.

The township of Munson, Ohio, replaced its Easter Egg Hunt with a Spring Egg Hunt in 2011. A compromise was to allow reference to Easter to remain if no taxpayers' money assisted the event.

Shortly before Easter 2011, Jessica, a sophomore at a private high school in Seattle, volunteered to assist a third-grade class in a local public school. Having heard about what she called "their abstract behaviour rules," she knew to ask the teacher's permission before suggesting the children fill little plastic eggs with treats, jelly beans, and candy. A mere teacher couldn't authorise such a thing. It was referred to the school administration. Graciously, the school allowed it, but only if they weren't called Easter Eggs. They were Spring Spheres.

The Seattle parks department allowed "egg hunts" that year. It just forbid all mention of Easter.

The seasons we celebrate aren't necessarily ours. In September 2012, the Australia and New Zealand Bank wished customers a Happy Mid-Autumn Festival. I didn't know what that was, but the wishes also expressed in Chinese meant it was something Chinese. September is autumn in China, but in Australia is spring. We mock our forebears who brought Europe to the Southern Hemisphere, but at least we realised the seasons had changed.

Eradicating our culture can only help other races retain theirs. Two months later, in November 2012, the bank told customers, *"Wishing you and your family a prosperous Diwali."* Having confirmed it referred to the Hindu Deepavali, at least I'd heard of it.

Not that the bank probably saw any of it as culture. It was business.

Where our companies go, our churches go too, with a better sense of the seasons. The penultimate Sunday in May 2015 was the Day of Pentecost, Whitsunday, but the sign outside Gordon Uniting Church made no mention of that. Instead, the church declared to people driving past that it was Autumn Festival. I think that was the year that the church ceased teaching Scripture in local schools.

In 2015, accountancy firm Grant Thornton wasn't mentioning Christmas, but it kindly wished me and others *"L'Shana Tova,"* a *"Happy Rosh Hashanah! Wishing you and your family a good and sweet new year and well over the Fast."* I didn't take offence for not being Jewish.

A Rasmussen poll late in 2010 found Americans preferred to be greeted "Merry Christmas" than "Happy Holidays," by sixty-nine to twenty-four percent; bland holidays haven't gelled. I'd rather think I'm wishing Europeans "Merry Christmas" and Jews "Happy Hanukah" getting it wrong a few times, than wish everyone "Happy Holidays" getting it wrong all the time.

16. THE RELIGION THAT HIDES

As we do, citizens of the Soviet Union treasured their rights. *"Freedom of religious worship and freedom of anti-religious propaganda is recognised for all citizens,"* provided article 124 of the 1936 constitution, which Soviet governments essentially honoured (unlike other provisions of Soviet constitutions). Anti-religious propaganda was all around, while religious propaganda was hard to find. Religious worship was secreted away.

Soviet communism remained avowedly atheistic, without political dissent or religious expression. No person joined the Communist Party of the Soviet Union and enjoyed the benefits reserved to party members without professing atheism, including Leonid Brezhnev. Born in 1906, he became general secretary of the Soviet Union in 1964. When he died in 1982, his widow bent over his body, kissed his forehead, and dabbed her tears away with a handkerchief. Their daughter kissed his face twice, before his coffin was closed.

Their actions were newsworthy for being the final ritual of the Russian Orthodox Church, at a time we thought Soviet rule had all but eradicated Christianity. The moving moment was a marked contrast with the political theatre around it. Religion is always more moving than politics.

It has become much the same in the West. The obliteration of our cultures by Western multiculturalism is never starker than in relation to religion, but much as Jewishness survives with reduced Jewish faith, so does Christendom with reduced Christian faith. Christianity bubbles beneath the new Western watch.

Outsiders mightn't have realised the connection, but the letters of the registration plates at the front and rear of the company cars of TNT Limited were the company's initials. When Holyman Limited came into being for being carved out from TNT, both companies wanted the registration plates changed for those cars transferring to Holyman. The Roads and Traffic Authority allocated new plates, but the finance director Reuben didn't want "*666*," the mark of the beast, for his car. As our shared secretary told me later, he flicked it to another company car: mine.

Holyman sold the car before the year was out. I never saw it or that plate again.

When I was young, Russia represented the evil cruel empire suppressing her people, while we imagined our West to be the beacon of freedom. Thirty years after Brezhnev's funeral, that's all turned around. Russia is one of the few beacons among European peoples. Her restored Christianity and rest of her culture might well be less than they were before the Great War and coming of communism, but they're more than most of the West retains.

Western welcoming of other cultures drives our cultures into hiding. My daughters suspected my eldest daughter's year-nine mathematics teacher, from Texas, was a Christian of faith, but she told a student: "Don't use words with religious connotations."

The student had responded to someone sneezing by saying "Bless you."

When a fellow student sneezed in her class in Dyer County, Tennessee in 2014, Kendra Turner also responded: "Bless you."

For that, Turner was suspended. Her teacher told her she would have no "godly speaking in class."

For other races, we relax our traditional rules and cultural norms. The Sikh religion requires boys not to cut their hair and to wear turbans, leading Ormiston College, a Christian school in Brisbane, to alter its dress code to accommodate a Sikh student in 2008. The school apologised for having previously tried to maintain it.

Compulsion in Sikhism and Islam give Sikhs and Muslims rights to wear Kara bracelets and hijabs throughout Britain. The Christian faith requires very little. That lack of religious compulsion allowed British Airways to dismiss Coptic Christian Nadia Eweida for wearing a Christian Cross visible at work. The Royal Devon and Exeter National Health Service Trust dismissed Shirley Chaplin, a thirty-one year veteran of nursing, for the same reason.

The more our liberties under God, the fewer our liberties under multiculturalism. Employers can dismiss people wearing Christian symbols, because we don't *have* to wear them. We might simply choose to do so. In 2012, the British government went so far as to argue before the European Court of Human Rights in Strasbourg *against* any right of Christians to wear Crosses at work.

Our determination to accommodate other races and their religions while riding roughshod over ours means it's hard not to feel the West is at war with Christianity. "In recent months the courts have refused to recognise the wearing of a Cross, belief in marriage between a man and a woman, and Sundays as a day of worship as core expressions of the Christian faith," complained Andrea Williams, director of the Christian Legal Centre, in 2012. "What next? Will our courts overrule the Ten Commandments?" Courts hadn't been asked.

Late in 2010, a Jewish mother at St Ives North Primary School complained to the New South Wales Department of Education that the class in which her child sat recognised Christmas trees. The class didn't recognise Jesus, or even Christmas, it seems, but merely Christmas trees. That, she wrote, made her children feel excluded.

What struck me about the complaint, when my wife told me about it, was a far more public controversy earlier that year. Christians had supported Jews wanting an eruv constructed through the streets of St Ives allowing Jews to feel they could venture outside on the Jewish Sabbath. An eruv is a make-believe wall denoted by wires, which allows Jews to pretend they're staying indoors. (If it were a make-believe beach, they could pretend to go swimming.)

I stopped supporting the eruv when I heard of that Jewish mother's complaint, and I thought about the Christian festivals that we can no longer publicly celebrate because they might make Jews and other races feel excluded. (That mightn't have been very noble of me, but there you are.) "*Religious faith belongs in people's hearts and homes and their places of worship,*" wrote John Watts (who I met) of St Ives to *The Sydney Morning Herald* newspaper. "*The streets, public space, should not become a religious battle ground. There must be no eruv poles and wires, and no religious symbols and paraphernalia beyond church or synagogue boundaries.*"

Western public places are no places for culture. Secularity becomes atheistic evangelism, or evangelical atheism, when it prevents people practicing their religion. All religions offend secularity: a polite word for prohibiting religion. Rather than just people of other religions feeling excluded, we can all feel excluded.

Simply because we've come to deem religion a private, personal affair, doesn't mean other races agree. For eight years, there'd been an eruv in Bondi. In 2015, Jews got permission for their eruv in St Ives.

Denying people the chance to express their tradition and storytelling in streets, schools, and shopping centres isn't just limiting for them. It's boring for others. We quarantine religion, as other races don't, sealing our customs peculiar to our people in private homes and churches, where people walking past can't see them.

Article 18 of the Universal Declaration of Human Rights in 1948 expressly extended rights to religious worship to both private and public places, but human rights are for other races' benefit. (We're supposedly so powerful in the present as not to need them and so wicked in the past as not to warrant them.) We defend and advance their religious rights, when salvaging ours might discomfort them.

Our freedom of religion is a freedom to be silent, to a faith we keep secret. Revealing Christianity has become offensive, much as revealing Judaism sometimes was. Other people's religions aren't our concern. Our religion is nobody's interest. We confine it to close chapel walls and the insides of our heads, where the rest of us aren't supposed to look.

Ours is the religion that hides. Western Christianity might be fading fast or dying altogether, but we can't see enough or hear enough to know.

In 2010, Senior Citizens, Inc. cited the separation of church and state (given federal grants to the elderly) when it told residents at the Ed Young Senior Citizens Centre at Port Wentworth, Georgia, they couldn't pray aloud before eating their meals. Instead, there was a moment of silence. In that silence, unspoken and unheard except by God, the old people could pray.

The best possible outcome for our religious pluralism, the only way not to offend, is silence. So much as harbouring thoughts towards God are better not mentioned.

Our local primary school's fortnightly newsletters included a small reference to the parents' prayer group among the community notices until 2012, when the school administrative officer banned reference to the group for fear of offending people of faiths other than Christianity. The prayer group was open to all faiths, but only Christians attended. In this case, the school headmistress didn't care enough to defy a determined parent, Luisa, pressing her on the issue, although the prayer group only occasionally reappeared in the newsletters. No longer was it a community notice, but among the advertisements.

The school repeatedly refused to publish advertisements for Scripture teachers; those at the school were Roman Catholic, Protestant, and Jewish. Nevertheless, in 2015 it published advertisements for ethics teachers.

Our right to anti-religious propaganda prevails over a right to religion. We're rarely keener for civil liberties than when it comes to atheists espousing atheism. Libertarians aren't satisfied to give people the right to join hell. They give them the right to bring others along for the ride.

Like citizens of the old Soviet Union, we have freedom to denigrate religion (well, Christianity anyway) we don't have to denigrate much else. Australian journalist Anthony Sharwood, an atheist, complained about *"God botherers"* like American footballer Tim Tebow praying on a football field. *"The fact is,"* he wrote in January 2012, *"there is something vulgar about wearing your religiousness on your sleeve… Get a room. Or more to the point, get a church."* Nobody was hurt, nobody affected, but Sharwood thought prayer wasn't just *"dumb."* It was *"religious fanaticism."*

Christianity had become religious fanaticism. It should be shut out of sight.

Other religions worn upon other races' sleeves didn't bother Sharwood. He liked it. *"Islam is an ancient, beautiful religion which is a welcome addition to our multicultural landscape,"* he wrote eleven months later, in December 2012.

We're not a country. We're a landscape.

Muslim prayers apparently aren't as vulgar, dumb, or fanatical as Christian prayers. Sharwood's Christian wife *"was in Turkey recently and was deeply moved by the daily sound of what she called 'ancient souls calling out to God'."*

Like our forefathers and mothers, the rest of the world doesn't treat religion as something so personal it should be hidden away. Religion fills people's lives, as it once filled ours. They're not as reticent as we are to call upon God.

We sense ancient souls better in other races than we sense ancient souls in ourselves. The souls that ancient Greek philosophers unfurled we sensed so freely only a generation or two ago, when we knew body and wondered what mind and religion might mean. Fewer and fewer people I've met through each year of my life reveal them, suggesting our souls aren't surviving through our isolation. Souls need society.

Cultural sensitivities don't remove all hints of Christianity from our educational institutions. Christianity comes out of hiding to be assaulted.

To facilitate discussion of the importance of symbols in culture, black American professor Deandre Poole (who taught Sunday school in church, he said) gave his class at Florida Atlantic University in March 2013 an exercise from the fifth edition of the textbook *Intercultural Communication: A Contextual Approach*. The students wrote the name *"Jesus"* in large letters on a piece of paper, placed it on the floor with the name facing up, and contemplated it. After a moment of silence, Poole told them to step on it.

When we treat our religion with disdain, we invite other races to do so as well, even those claiming the faith. In spite of the controversy, the university renewed Poole's contract. We tolerate contempt for Christianity unimaginable about other faiths. If people dare mention Christ, they do so to reject Him.

I'd looked forward to a representative from the Jews for Jesus organisation addressing our parish Anglican church the last Sunday evening of November 2009. Certain that Jews couldn't be for Jesus, I relished the prospect of challenging such a contradiction.

Even better than that, I learnt I'd been wrong. Mark was a Jew for Jesus because he was racially a Jew, who knew Christ to be the Son of God. He lived by Jewish ritual and culture, more than any other Jew I knew, fulfilled by Christian conviction and more ritual. He was a Christian Jew, the noun being his race, not a Jewish Christian. Seeing Christianity as the fulfilment of Judaism was a rationally cogent culture the like of which I'd rarely encountered.

Being a Christian European is no longer so logically coherent. We've lost our nexus to religious expression, even if we choose to participate. We imagine retaining our faith apart from our culture, but religious meaning and body come from practices along with beliefs. The West is losing both. I bought some of the books Mark was selling.

No Muslim or Jew ever offended me by declaring his or her faith. The third Friday in August 2015, I sat among a hundred and thirty other guests attending a service and dinner at a synagogue (a real synagogue, not an eruv).

We might respect people of other races and religions far more by asserting our faiths in our countries, as they assert theirs in their countries and ours. Concealing our faiths disrespects God and us.

17. OUR LANDS OF OTHER FAITHS

"Give me the children until they are seven and anyone may have them afterwards," said sixteenth-century missionary Saint Francis Xavier. The kingdom of Navarre, where he was born in 1506, became part of the recently formed union of Spain in 1512. He was a founder of the Society of Jesus, the Jesuit order, training children to think. He proselytised to the world but, for all his well-meaning effort, died alone on an island in China.

Saint Francis' words didn't lend themselves well to a maxim. The Jesuit maxim became "Give me a child until he is seven, and I will give you the man."

Our latter-day West focuses our efforts on matters altogether different to Saint Francis, before we each die alone. When we turn our minds to religion, we care less about the faith of our forebears than of other people's forebears. With responsibility upon us to make multiculturalism work, the religions we teach are everyone else's.

On the last Wednesday in November 2010, my eldest daughter was part of a school excursion to the Chinese Gardens in Sydney. There, the children learnt about sacred fish.

St John's Presbyterian Church established the Wahroonga Preparatory School for the littlest of children in 1926. Five decades later, I sat my first two years of school there, standing to sing 'God Save The Queen.' Without knowing so then, we were the last vestiges of Christendom. "*As a Uniting Church School,*" the school's website declared another four decades later, "*Wahroonga Preparatory School will promote Christian faith and values explicitly and implicitly through its attitudes and actions, whilst at the same time respecting other religious beliefs.*"

We do more than respect them. We promote them. In September 2011, I had returned to the school with my sons. Hanging in the air in the years-five and six classroom were images of Buddha.

My wife and daughters were at the Willoughby Street Fair, where the girl guides of their troop were rare participants not Chinese, before an overwhelmingly Chinese crowd. Again, there was Buddha.

With Western churches espousing cultural equality in place of Christian conviction, Christianity wanes, but people want something in which to believe. People turn to those cultures in which their respective race or races have confidence and to religions offering conviction.

Religions offering certainty flourish. Conviction prevails over confusion and inclusion. Collective conviction is more persuasive than the flimsy resolves of individualist Christians.

Without thought of religion or religious discrimination I'm sure, Australian airline Virgin Blue in 2006 unabashedly recruited only people who believed in karma (according to a presenter to my last management conference at Cement Australia). Thankfully, it excluded pilots from that requirement.

Karma is among the most popular selections from our smorgasbord of religions and bits of them. It offers meaning without structures and discipline: godlike without godly rules. We decide what's nice and what's not. In a lovely construct of the universe, we construe rewards when we're looking for affirmation of what we're doing or have done. We don't incur punishments, but see suffering in other people's lives when we want to condemn them. It's individual self-interest, cloaked in the guise of some kind of spiritual belief: a reason for self-centred individuals to be nice in the expectation we'll benefit, without attempting to fathom why we should.

Our faith isn't in karma. It's in people and religions not ours. The West doesn't try to understand anything about Buddhism, Hinduism, or any other religion incorporating karma. We don't wonder how karma could possibly be real.

"I believe in karma," Ray told me, the second last day he came to our home installing new gutters in 2011. "Do you believe in karma?"

"No," I told him. "It hasn't been my experience."

Ray was normally chatty, too chatty, but he quickly ended that conversation. "Aah, well," he said, "you and I are different."

He might've presumed I had no reason to be nice if I didn't believe in karma. He thus had no reason to be nice to me. He never did finish clearing away the bracket around an old downpipe he'd removed near our front door.

Attendees at the Grace Hopper Celebration of Women in Computing conference in Phoenix in October 2014 weren't so confident in karma. Women were being paid generally less money than men, but Microsoft chief executive and Indian immigrant Satya Nadella told them they shouldn't ask for more. "...the system will actually give you the right raises as you go along...because that's good karma." The outcry compelled him to apologise.

The West embraces without question other race's religions for no other reason than they're other race's religions. We don't scrutinise those religions as we criticise ours.

My lawyer friend Garry made no mention of Christmas 2009. Two months later, he delighted in Chinese New Year and the coming Year of the Tiger.

By 2010, Christmas and Easter no longer existed at my eldest daughter's high school. Her Chinese teacher celebrated Chinese New Year by handing out little red envelopes with Chinese characters.

A few years earlier, a newspaper website didn't publish my comment contrasting its enthusiasm for the lunar calendar with its indifference to Christmas. In Australia, Chinese New Year gets better airplay.

Amidst the frenzy of Chinese New Year, every detail of Chinese astrology is reported in the news as if it were real, with no one so vulgar as to say otherwise. In year seven, my middle-born daughter began her second week of compulsory classes in Chinese by being taught in great detail the Chinese zodiac. All religions are equal should mean all astrology is equal, but newspapers report Chinese astrology at the front end of the news while women's magazines publish horoscopes and other Western astrology at the back, albeit as if they too were real.

By January 2014, "Happy New Year" in Sydney meant the Chinese New Year. The Asian calendar was replacing ours, but we'd begun dismantling ours years earlier. Dates before Christ, B.C., had become B.C.E., replacing Christ with the Common or Current Era, whatever that is. We're no longer *anno Domini*.

"I am technically Church of England," said former London mayor Ken Livingstone in 2005, but "I became an atheist by the time I was eleven. I rejected all this mumbo jumbo in favour of rational science."

Neither rational science nor atheism deters the West from other races' religions. While campaigning for the 2012 mayoral election, Livingstone told the North London Central Mosque that he wanted to "educate the mass of Londoners" in Islam. "That will help to cement our city as a beacon that demonstrates the meaning of the words of the prophet... I want to spend the next four years making sure that every non-Muslim in London knows and understands" Mohammed's "words and message."

No candidate promised to ensure everyone in London knew and understood Christianity. That would be disrespectful.

There is little, if any, postmodern Judaism and no postmodern Islam like postmodern Christianity. There's no multicultural Islam or Judaism like multicultural Christianity, imagining a single theistic religion for all, but we're too busy embracing them to notice.

In 2010, the British Broadcasting Corporation was surprised to learn that Islamic schools in Britain hadn't redefined Islam the way we'd redefined Christianity. They teach their children that people who don't follow Islam will be subject to hellfire in death. (We used to think people not following Christ were denied eternal life, when we had only the Bible to go on.)

Muslims still believe Islam. So can we.

Part of the process by which Christians overcome our faith, what really excited Robert Beckford in his 2007 dissertation *The Hidden Story of Jesus* was the Gospel of Thomas, found in Egypt in 1945. Dating from around the time of the canonical Gospels, it was allegedly a collection of Jesus' sayings. Many of them repeated those in the Gospels. Some were new. Most importantly for Beckford, there was no mention of His virgin birth or Resurrection. To the Cairo museum assistant he asked about it, and so by inference to all sensible Christians, the Gospel of Thomas was devastating.

Television can be frustrating when we watch such jaundiced stupidity and can't call out, "Don't be ridiculous!" If indeed the Gospel of Thomas is a collection of Jesus' sayings, then that's all it is. It has no impact on sensible Christians of faith, but I'd stopped believing Beckford was sensible. He was a theologian.

Beckford spoke fondly of the reverence Muslims supposedly give Jesus (although clearly not Christians), claiming God pulled

Him away before the Crucifixion so that a man looking like Him was crucified. (I couldn't imagine why God would do that.) Apparently awaiting Jesus in a Muslim holy city is a burial place because Muslims believe He will come again to be buried beside Mohammed. They think Jesus was a very nice fellow but not the Son of God. Neither does the West, anymore.

In 2001, a large Muslim population meant the school district in Dearborn, Michigan, began closing schools for Islamic holy days. Ten years later, the school system's communications co-ordinator David Mustonen wrote that *"people have come to realize that it is no different than taking time off at Christmas or Easter."*

In 2010, public schools in Burlington, Vermont began closing on *Eid al-Fitr* due to their increasing Muslim population. Dan Balon, director of the school district's diversity and equity office, said the district decided to close rather than risk low attendance rates by forcing students to choose between school and staying home to celebrate the holiday.

In 2011, schools in Cambridge, Massachusetts began closing for one Muslim holiday each year: either *Eid al-Fitr* or *Eid al-Adha*, the Festival of Sacrifice, depending on which day falls within the school year. If both fell within the school year, the schools closed for one of the days.

Saudi Arabia funded a field trip by Wellesley Middle School sixth-grade students to a Boston mosque in May 2010; no one asserts a separation of mosque and state. During a prayer service, they knelt.

Instead of learning about other people's religions knowing they're other people's religions, we affirm them as we're unwilling to defend ours. We don't need to know or understand them. (It's better if we don't.)

Dawah is the propagation of Islam. "There is no truth except Allah," sang students of Grand Junction High School, Colorado in 2012, part of Indian composer A.R. Rahman's song *'Zikr'*.

"This is about bringing diversity to the students and showing them other things that are out there," explained school spokesman Jeff Kirtland. "The teacher was open with the parents, and students do not have to participate in this voluntary club choir."

James Harper withdrew from the choir, but a Christian active in church isn't the diversity the West wants. There was no suggestion of the choir not singing the song because one person disagreed, although we ceased Christmas and Easter commemorations if one person objected.

Mere mention of Christianity to other races is culturally insensitive, while embracing their religions gives us new perspectives. It gives us theirs.

The cultural sensitivities that meant our local primary school barred children from sharing Christmas candy canes didn't deter it from conducting an excursion of stage-two children (years three and four, encompassing children aged eight, nine, and ten) to the Auburn Gallipoli Mosque the second Monday in August 2010. They were *"learning about people and their beliefs,"* although that no longer allowed excursions to a church.

The school went so far as to suggest parents pack their children's lunches *"with a Turkish flair,"* whatever that meant. It presumably didn't mean massacring Armenians.

There were no letters to parents to say the excursion wouldn't occur if anyone felt offended; we're not pandering to white people's intolerance. Luisa, the mother of my second son's friend Ben, was uncomfortable with the excursion but, like my wife, knew that mentioning it to the school would disadvantage her son. Christians of faith prove far more tolerant of atheists and other religions than atheists and other religions tolerate Christians.

Not that we care. Noticing would be prejudice.

Christmas messages broadcast by Western television stations no longer need to be about Christmas. They can be pleas for tolerance, but not for Christianity. They can also be abuse, but only of Christians.

The 2006 Christmas address on Britain's Channel 4 was from a British-born Muslim woman abusing House of Commons leader Jack Straw for speaking out against Muslim women in Britain wearing veils. She was never identified, concealed as she was by a veil.

In 2008, the world's financial markets were in turmoil. Other Christmas messages pleaded for calm, but not that on Britain's Channel 4. Iran's President Mahmoud Ahmadinejad had repeatedly threatened to destroy Israel and led a uranium enrichment programme to build nuclear weapons, but in his Christmas message decried the "bullying, ill-tempered, and expansionist" British and Americans.

Ahmadinejad insisted that, were Jesus alive, he too would

oppose the British and Americans. With all we've done to redefine Christ, Muslims can too. Besides, we'd reached the same conclusion. Meanwhile, Iran executed Iranians converting to Christianity.

With white people so keen to abuse our lesser selves, we invite other races to abuse us too, and broadcast it. (Critics claimed ratings motivated Channel 4.) A year earlier, Ahmadinejad's invitation to Britons to appear on Iranian television hadn't been for them to abuse Iranians. He paraded fifteen captured British sailors and marines he said had strayed into Iranian waters.

Swedish Television's annual Christmas Eve celebration is a major event. In 2015, the hostess was a young Muslim Arab woman, Gina Dirawi.

The West loves Muslims. More than eleven thousand athletes participated in the 2016 Olympic Games at Rio de Janeiro, but the only one I read of *"winning hearts everywhere"* (in the words of the *Huffington Post* website) did so before she'd competed. She was Ibtihaj Muhammad, the first Olympian representing America to wear a hijab.

When we don't want other religions confronting us, we're being insensitive, feeling unjustified prejudice. When people of other religions don't want our religion confronting them, they're being sensitive, feeling justified offence.

George Washington University Law School professor John Banzhaf can't have thought all religions were the same. In 2015, he complained to the Washington Office of Human Rights that there were *"too many crosses in every room of Catholic University"* in Washington, which was a *"human rights violation that prevents Muslim students from praying there."* His sixty-page complaint described the Catholic imagery as *"offensive."*

The races replacing us need not be Christian. Our churches need not remain churches.

In Germany, churches are becoming mosques. "One thing is for sure," Chancellor Angela Merkel told the Frankfurter *Allgemeine Zeitung* in 2010, "our country will continue to change, and integration is a duty for a society that welcomes immigrants." Thus, "mosques, among other things, will become an ever-more present feature of our landscape." Mosques belong in Germany because synagogues have since 1945.

A West refusing to distinguish one culture from another, one religion from another, cannot see the change in a German church becoming another race's religious building. Other races see it. Their religious leaders support them. Ours support them too.

No longer the Christian West and no longer interested in the truth or our salvation, there is no reason why we should not be Muslim or anything else. The West's dogmatic determination not to distinguish between races and religions makes our post-Christian Christendom indistinguishable from an Islamic caliphate. Church bells rarely ringing anymore become antiquated equivalents to Muslim calls to prayer.

Islam requires Muslims to pray but does not specify the times or places they should do so. Thus when Muslims block cars and pedestrians to pull out their prayer mats and kneel upon them across the West as they do not across their countries, they are asserting themselves and their cultures as we refuse to defend us and ours.

In 2019, the Municipal Board in Bromölla, Sweden banned all prayer during working hours. The ban applied to all religions, but only Muslims were demanding rights to pray at work. Thus the Discrimination Ombudsman became involved. In 2020, the administrative court in Malmö insisted employers must allow Muslims to roll out their prayer mats in the workplace during working hours and to kneel in prayer to Allah.

Islam does not require Muslims to pray at work. Multiculturalism encourages it.

"If you ... go and serve other gods and bow down to them," Joshua told the Israelites at Chapter 23, verse 16 of the Book of Joshua, "the Lord's anger will burn against you, and you will quickly perish from the good land he has given you."

The Jersey City Board of Education didn't close schools for Jewish holidays Rosh Hashanah or Yom Kippur, but when it voted in 2015 not to close them for *Eid al-Adha*, Muslims were furious. "We're going to be the majority soon," pointedly declared one Muslim parent.

18. HOLY MOTHERS

If we saw the world of human beings and relationships instead of political power and commercial transactions, we'd realise how matriarchal we were. When fathers became sick, family life continued. When mothers became sick, family life struggled. Children took the religion of their mothers.

Nothing made our forebears prouder than the homes they made, families they kept. My father described expectant mothers as being "great with child." Whether he meant merely physical enlargement or much more, I've come to feel the same.

Much changed after my parents' generation. My mother insisted she didn't hate anything, but she disliked intensely the British television comedy series *Some Mothers Do 'Ave 'Em*. Frank Spencer was a good-hearted fool, but a fool nevertheless: a bumbling moron. My mother called the programme, for the title it carried, "an insult to motherhood."

She countered any rudeness or other cruel remark about another person by saying that other person was somebody's child. Every adult began life an infant in a crib, a vulnerable small boy or girl. Seeing other people in terms of their births and childhoods can make us nicer people. It's no reason to excuse wrongdoing or tolerate the intolerable in adults, but is cause to pause before rushing to hate them. It can make parents the nicest people.

Roman Catholic churches remain distinctive for their glorious white statues and other representations of the Holy Mother. Not idols, they are warm, fond affections.

Tucked into the chapel of our parish Anglican church (so Anglo-Catholic), with her head bowed in prayer, is a white marble effigy of an angel, as large as a person. "*In Memory of a Little Mother*," records the plaque on the base. I don't know what it means.

For centuries on each fifteenth day of August, Roman Catholics celebrated the Feast of the Assumption of Mary, commemorating the Holy Mother's body rising to heaven after Her earthly death. In 2008, for the first time so far as any of us parishioners were aware, our parish Anglican church convened a service for the Order of the Holy Eucharist for the Blessed Virgin Mary.

Old Father John, his hair whiter than the angel statue out of sight, delivered the sermon that Friday evening. He'd given some of the worst sermons I'd heard in church (one with talk of all religions being the same), but that night he bound the tiny congregation with words more profound than most I've heard. "With the Reformation we removed a lot of things we should have removed from the Catholic Church," he said, or words to that effect, in a church part of the denomination King Henry VIII founded. "With our rush to do so, we removed some things we should have kept. One of those was our deference for the Virgin Mary."

Deference to Mary is deference to motherhood. God choosing Mary to bear His Holy Child made Her the Holy Mother: holy by reason of being a mother. Joseph wasn't the Child's father in the ordinary sense, but theirs were the earthly lines to which the Holy Child was born.

Paintings of the Madonna and Child were the most beautiful from the collection of fifteenth and sixteenth-century Italian paintings in the *Accademia Carrara* in Bergamo, which dominated a Renaissance art exhibition at the National Gallery of Australia to which I took my three eldest children. The images evolved with our evolving sense of the Holy Mother and Baby through the ages: from being regal and aloof through being more common but still separated from us by a balustrade, until Titian painted Them on our side of a balustrade.

Celebrating Mary celebrates motherhood: She exquisitely feminine, Her Baby boldly boyish but vulnerable. They loved and would uphold the Other.

What Protestants diminished with the Reformation, the West lost with individualism. In 2012, the Roman Catholic Church tried to save Australian women wanting to marry from missing out by suggesting they marry young because of the shortage of good income earning, single men as they became older. Some wise heads counselled them from rushing into wrong choices. More commonplace were quick rebukes. "*How dare the church tells us what to do*," wrote Lorissa. "*It's our life so we will live it how we want. We won't we told how to live it.*" Her typographical error might've resulted from her fury as she typed.

We who'd venerated parenthood no longer do. Some of our schools ceased recognising Mother's Day and Father's Day for fear of excluding children without mothers or fathers. We ceased celebrating parenthood for fear of excluding people without children. For all our talk of inclusion, we exclude parenthood.

Between my Christmas times in London in 1986 and '96, I was struck at how much the shop window displays had lost their childishness through those ten intervening years. They'd become adult. When we removed the Christian story from Christmas, we lost the instant in history when the universe centred upon a single birth. We lost the power and magnificence of infancy.

A woman is never more powerful than in becoming a mother. A man never stands taller than in becoming a father. The West didn't need to lose our love for childbearing because we lost Christianity, but we lost it anyway.

Not all of us with faith understand. People deliberately not bearing children can still be good people. Sometimes, good people make mistakes.

I hadn't imagined there were too many Benedictine monks left in the world, until I encountered Brother Ned Gerber. I'd also thought only Roman Catholics could be Christian monks. Ned, like his brother, was an Anglican Benedictine. Ned's sermon for Christmas Day 2014 at our parish Anglican church wasn't about asylum seekers or Muslim girls' education but, strangely, the birth of Christ. He pointed out that the Virgin Mary was probably a teenager. God making her the Holy Mother venerated youth.

Ned wasn't as portly as monks should be, although the black robes and tussocks he donned for Sunday morning services made seem him a little larger than he was. They didn't make him seem older, and he looked much younger than his fifty-six years when first we'd met, more than half a decade earlier. He'd worn a suit, shirt, and tie to lead the services Sunday evenings, as he wore them through the week. Ned may well have been the only monk working as a finance accountant for one of the world's largest accountancy firms and then the healthcare industry.

He was a "normal red-blooded male," he told me, with a broad grin across his face. Ned justified his monastic vow of celibacy on two grounds.

The first was the Apostle Paul having been called by God to be celibate (although Paul might already have been a widower and even a father when God called him). Historians credit the zealous Paul with being one of the two people most responsible for Christianity spreading after Jesus' Crucifixion. Historians without Christian faith could arguably make Paul the most responsible.

"With the greatest respect," I told Ned, "you're not Paul."

Sounding much like a man without faith, Ned went onto say he could do things without a family he couldn't do with one. (If Adam and Eve felt that way, there'd have been no Cain, Abel, or anyone else.) "I work eighty hours a week," he told me.

"You shouldn't," I told him, as I'd say to anyone working eighty hours a week, especially in finance.

"I can fly off to Africa." His Benedictine order operated a hospital saving Africans. "I can visit Anke in Hong Kong, on my way back from Chicago." Anke was a sick Chinese woman.

He could've done it all with a family, if he'd wanted to. Ned lacked the balance and proportion that only children quick to put us in our places provide. His celibacy made bearing life's pitfalls much harder than bearing them would've been with a family to ground him; God would've been there in both events. A God-given family could've ameliorated his stress of a former church secretary (not a parishioner) filing an official complaint against him, as she complained of several people. Many a time, I've drawn comfort through difficult situations with thoughts of my family.

The first Saturday in December 2010, I was again in the town hall that twenty-four years earlier had been the church hosting my mother's funeral. A Christian choir performed the cantata *Son of David*, after which I met Joy from Camden over supper. Her husband Bruce was in the choir. Conversation turned to children, as it easily could with six of mine around us. "Are you a Mum?" I would've asked.

She wasn't. When I asked her about it, she told me she'd been a nun for twenty-one years after leaving school.

Her answer took me aback. I had a question I thought more interesting than asking why she'd *become* a nun. "Why did you cease being a nun?"

Her reply dumbfounded me. "I became a Christian."

"That's not the most obvious answer."

Being a nun is a structure of rules, she explained. Celibacy, she said, "wasn't natural." What's natural, she said, is procreation.

Christianity does much to realise our racial natures (as other religions do for their races). Celibacy denies us something of human nature. By the time Joy married Bruce she was, at least in those days, too old for them to become parents. She suffered a miscarriage, and never carried a child full term.

Monks, nuns, and Roman Catholic clergy aside, Western people of faith bear more children than those without it. We don't bear enough.

Researcher Eric Kaufmann reported that ninety-seven percent of the world's population growth in 2010 was among religious people. Mormons and conservative evangelicals in America had nearly twice the birth rate of irreligious Americans. In Europe, white women who regularly attended church bore up to half a child more on average than irreligious women of the same education level. Within all races, the religious bear more children than the irreligious, but fewer white people than people of other races retain religion. Removing our religion reduced our childbearing.

My father described marriage as "the benefit of clergy." Without religion, white people have no churches in which to make friends and lovers. I met the woman who later became my wife in church.

If individualism and the decline of Christianity don't deter us from marriage, they contribute to marriage breakdown. Believing in a perfect God makes us accept imperfect people. (We should never confuse a perfect God with imperfect Christians or an imperfect Church.)

Without faith in God, white people presume their individual selves are close to perfect (however horrible we think the rest of our races are). They expect their spouses to be closer still. We're more tolerant of other races than we are of our spouses' imperfections, much as our spouses are intolerant of ours.

With our six children, my wife and I have become rare among Western people. Sitting together in our parish Anglican church on Maundy Thursday 2012, we comprised about a fifth of the congregation. Feeling proud for my family filling a rear pew beside me, I was struck by the sense that people choosing not to bear children lack self-love.

The only child with more siblings at our children's primary school through our time there, whose parents we never saw, was Aqduss: a Muslim, the youngest of eight children. Half a year after finishing school, my middle-born daughter learnt that Aqduss had already married.

Higher birth rates among Muslims have allowed Islam to overtake Roman Catholicism as the largest religious denomination on earth. In the tally not just of people but faiths, we're losing.

Aside from my children, most of the children attending kids club at our parish Anglican church each Wednesday afternoon after school were Asians. Their parents took advantage of childcare costing only ten dollars a term. Family conscious as they were, parents came to church to see their children in nativity plays, but not otherwise. Kids club soon folded. Nativity plays ended.

For several years, I sat among the good men and women of the church fête committee. Most of the parishioners retired from their jobs but never the church, making cakes, jams, lemon butter, and sometimes coconut ice. (I really like coconut ice.) A stall sold tea cosies knitted by the residents of a nearby nursing home, but the hardware stall ended when the men operating it became too aged and too few people had old tools to donate. That first year without their stall, the men donated money.

The houses our old people leave to enter nursing homes are becoming apartments, so somebody on the committee suggested marketing the fête to those residents. "They're all Asian," retorted the committee chairman Bill, a semi-retired engineer and businessmen by then working only two days a week.

Two parishioners in 2008 funded a small farm and parishioners in other years donated other attractions, desperately trying to entice children to come. The fête is more challenging each year. The time will come there'll be no fête, no lace and linen stall. Sometime thereafter, there'll be no church.

God doesn't dissipate without Christians. Faiths disappear without the faithful to believe them.

"Latvians understand that in fifty years this will be an Islamic state," the head of the Riga mosque, Ahmed Robert Klimovičs, told Latvia's *Morning Independent* newspaper in October 2015. "This is because Islamic children will be in the majority." He had three children so far, saying he and other Muslims "are working to have more" in an effort to colonise the country sooner. "If people come here who practice Islam, God will prevent them from integrating into your society, where everything is permissible... I am categorically against integration."

We dismiss such declarations without thought of the future, but empires of people prevail over empires left without them. The future will be theirs in one all-conquering regard.

19. ENVIRONMENTALISM

"All things bright and beautiful,
  "All creatures great and small,
  "All things wise and wonderful,
  "The Lord God made them all."

The nineteenth-century hymn known by British children the world over was unknown to my children until I mentioned it, although my fifteen-year-old eldest son recognised the second line as the name of a British television series. He'd never seen the show but it featured actor Peter Davison, who later become an incarnation of the television character, the Doctor.

The hymn reflected our long history of conserving our natural environment. Like us, lush green forests and waterways were beautiful. We wanted fresh water to wash around our mouths, clean air for our lungs to breathe. Bright red robins and sprightly brown squirrels were joys to behold.

People defending their beautiful neighbourhoods are exercising self-interests intrinsically rational and reasonable. Accompanying my father to see local residents protesting plans for a freeway through South Turramurra bushland, around about 1987, I watched them applaud speeches about the evils of motor cars. They then climbed into their cars for their short journeys home.

Communists in government in Eastern Europe until 1989 were preoccupied with rampant production, dismissing environmental concerns for being bourgeois. With the coming of democracy, they woke quickly to people's most obvious individual interests, such as being able to breathe and drink water.

Without gods or God of one's own, the next big thing is a galactic environment. More than merely caring for our natural environment, the West progressed from environmental conservation into strict environmentalism.

People who don't so much as raise an eyebrow for somebody else obediently switch off all electricity and segregate garbage into different coloured bins, because we're told doing so saves the environment. We who refuse to countenance societies, families, or God suggesting what we do, faithfully accede to the pronouncements of people and bodies declaring the environment their mission: a sort of environmental infallibility. We trustingly accept without question the dictate of an undefined, omnipotent, and omnipresent Mother Earth.

The economics that compels so much of the West doesn't deter us from spending money on trees. The costs of building a busway three kilometres through Brisbane ballooned by several million dollars in 2008, because of tunnelling to preserve a "much loved" tree with local heritage significance. Queensland's Premier Anna Bligh said the tree "is highly valued by the local community."

Governments normally commission studies not to find the truth, but to verify what they already think is the truth. Early in the new millennium, the British government commissioned a study to prove that cloth nappies were environmentally better than disposable nappies. Instead, the study found that the repeated use of detergent with cloth nappies made them more environmentally damaging than disposable nappies. Rather than upset people using cloth nappies on environmental grounds, the government suppressed the report.

The purpose of environmentalism isn't to help the environment. It's to comfort people into thinking they're helping the environment.

The West's comprehensive embracing of environmentalism demonstrates our need for religion of some form or another. For all our talk of liberty, we want limits upon endless liberties. We desperately want disciplines: the structures of society. Environmentalism is a multicultural perspective, ideal for a West that rejects talk of nation, race, and traditional religions. We think globally, and nothing's more global than the environment, short of God.

Like our other postmodern religions, environmentalism draws upon our religious heritage. The great flood covering the earth in the 2014 American film *Noah* (written and directed by Darren Aronofsky, an atheist Jew) flowed not from human immorality, as it does in the Bible, but from our neglect for the environment. God never rated a mention.

Environmentalism offers eternity, or something towards it: interests in the universe after we die. People who couldn't care less about the day after tomorrow fret themselves silly about sea levels in seven hundred years' time. Philip, the father of a friend to my eldest daughter, told me at a school parents' gathering that made climate change the most important problem facing the world.

I'd first heard the theory that human activity emitting carbon dioxide was warming the Earth much like a greenhouse warms plants in the late 1980s. I thought the stakes were high enough to warrant investigation and reasonable response, before I appreciated the West's eagerness for unreasonable response. When the Earth didn't warm, our language altered seamlessly from global warming to climate change.

Whether human activity affects climate and, if so, the extent of those effects should be a question of scientific discovery, about which reasonable people seeking truth might disagree. Instead, it's another edict by which we prove our environmentalist credentials.

Postmodernism doesn't pertain to environmental issues. There's no relativism but only facts, unquestionable and absolute. It's our prefect crusade, providing new-found certainty and conviction with the zeal of old-world missionaries among the unwashed. Science we've dismissed when it comes to human biology, we cite over and over to support the environment. Scientists are suddenly important again.

We don't need all scientists to agree. We just need them to say they agree. Kim, the Golden Cross Resources chief executive, knew a scientist among those on a published list of scientists stating emphatically that human activity was changing the Earth's climate, but Kim knew the scientist to be undecided on the issue. He told Kim that he needed to put his name to the list or the Australian government would withhold four million dollars funding his research into other matters.

If climate fears were based simply on science, then scientists would be free not to believe the theory. They are not.

The scientific method was traditionally based upon observation and data. There is less traditional science behind fears that human activity is changing the climate in any material and detrimental way than most people realise.

In terms of the future, there is primarily modelling of what will happen according to various probabilities. Predictive modelling can be logical, but if the events forecast do not eventuate, the model ought to be reviewed and perhaps adjusted or abandoned. Perhaps it is adjusted, but people wedded to the cause seem only to make excuses for predictions failing to occur, or ignoring those failures altogether. More dire predictions of the future replaced predictions failing to prove true.

Most importantly, if climate fears were based simply on science, then scientists with observations, data, and logical conclusions that contradict the theory could publish papers about it, contributing to discussion and debate. They are not free to publish them.

Waiting to board the mining industry cruise on Sydney Harbour, the cold and wet second Friday of July 2010, an elderly chemical engineer from Sydney University described to me a conversation he had had with a scientist who'd analysed carbon levels in the Antarctic ice. "He told me that no matter how many times he goes back to the ice, he gets the same results. The Earth isn't warming at all. It's cooling, and has been for the last two years. He says we're coming into another Ice Age, but he can't publish any papers about it."

The engineer began frantically shaking his head. "The only people getting government money are ones saying the Earth is warming, and it's all human activity causing it."

The peer review process once ensured that published academic papers were intellectually sound. It now ensures those papers are politically correct.

Increasingly since the Second World War, our purpose in science has ceased being to determine the facts. It has been to affirm what we believe facts should be: science not to pursue knowledge, but defend it. It's science as a matter of faith (science from a Muslim perspective). We're happy to frighten each other silly about environmental issues, as we refuse about other races and religions.

Environmentalism fulfils our Western dream of a single world religion superseding traditional religions, with a particular liking for the most primitive peoples. For Native Americans, environmental issues reflect their traditional religions. Unlike us, they're willing to espouse them.

Costa Rican Christiana Figueres, executive secretary of the United Nations Framework Convention on Climate Change, invoked the ancient Mayan jaguar goddess Ixchel in her speech at the climate negotiations in Cancun, Mexico in November 2010. Not merely the goddess of the moon, Ixchel was also "the goddess of reason, creativity, and weaving." Of the goddess of so much, Figueres told delegates, "May she inspire you."

The only people to rival the West in creating and conferring rights are American Indians. Their capacity to do so has no limit.

Bolivia, with a large indigenous population, elected Latin America's first indigenous president, Evo Morales, in 2006. In 2008, his entourage distributed a pamphlet at the United Nations setting out his ten "*commandments*" to save the planet, commencing with the need "*to end capitalism.*"

In January 2011, Bolivia enacted the Law of the Rights of Mother Earth, granting the earth rights to life, water, and clean air, as well as to repair livelihoods affected by human activities and to be free from pollution. Bugs, trees and all other natural things have the same rights as humans. In spite of its abundant natural resources, called "*blessings*," Bolivia remained one of the poorest countries in Latin America, at least for people.

A few months later, Bolivia tabled a draft United Nations treaty deeming the earth a living entity and accusing human beings of trying to "*dominate and exploit*" the planet. "*Mother Earth has the right to exist, to persist and to continue the vital cycles, structures, functions and processes that sustain all human beings.*" The "*severe destruction*" caused by humans was "*offensive to the many faiths, wisdom traditions, and indigenous cultures for whom Mother Earth is sacred.*"

The treaty would have established a Ministry of Mother Earth, with an ombudsman to hear nature's complaints. In the West, that might've meant talking to trees, but we already know what nature wants.

Morales was Roman Catholic, but also held the Andean belief in an earth deity known as Pachamama, the centre of life, by which human beings are equal to other entities. Andean environmentalism expresses their religion, as it's evolved in the circumstances around them.

Native American environmentalism advances their tribes, while rejecting the West. So does Western environmentalism, never far from the rest of our self-loathing.

In October 2012, my second daughter told me of a short film her high school had shown her and other students. In it, two unpleasant white people dismissed any need to care for the natural environment, while an Asian spoke of our need to care for it and a Muslim spoke of human activity changing the Earth's climate.

We can't bring ourselves to cast ill upon other races or to feel good about ours, but no race on earth does more than we do to protect the environment; it's hard to see most of the world doing much at all. While we fret in fear that carbon dioxide is warming the planet, an Arab sheikh in 2008 flew his Lamborghini sports car to London for a service; perhaps he couldn't get good service in Qatar. The outcry in Britain wasn't against Muslims or Arabs but rich people in general, in spite of rich Europeans being the most passionate supporters of measures to reduce industrial emissions of carbon dioxide.

Oil-producing Arabian Gulf emirates build snowfields in the desert and cool the sands, without regard for carbon emissions. Middle Eastern and Asian countries protested the European Union's imposition of carbon taxes on international airlines. Their environmental actions are adjuncts to their national interests. China promotes the solar panels it sells. Israel avoids dependence on oil to avoid dependence on Arabs.

We don't notice we're primarily the people trying so virtuously to save African elephants, Brazilian rainforests, and so forth; that would be racist. Besides, naturalist David Suzuki is Canadian Japanese. Hindu Indians hold cows to be sacred. The natural environment enjoys not just Native Americans but also the West defending it.

John Pearman, a retired university lecturer, described himself as "one of Australia's leading environmental warriors." Unmarried, childless, and living alone, he might've expected to die leaving no evidence he'd lived, until he built a house to be a model for environmentally sustainable living. The thick soil and long, unkempt grass across the roof were natural insulation from outside heat and cold. To support the great weight, the foundations of the house needed to be thick concrete pylons. In John's words, they could support a seven-storey building. He blamed them on an overzealous architect.

The Earth could fall into the sun with every other human record obliterated. John's house will survive.

Most of us aren't so thoughtful. The Queen's Birthday long weekend 2009, in which my eldest son and I saw the film *Collateral*, was the second annual Making Your Mark long weekend of what the Channel Ten television network called *"environmental programming,"* in a media release the previous Thursday. Nothing mentioned Her Majesty, but several programmes included environmental segments and story lines. The film *Collateral* wasn't one of them, but we saw public announcements about people supposedly marking a mark.

They weren't marking marks. Somebody didn't use shopping bags. A group of people removed a school's carbon footprint. Marking a mark in the West had become not marking a mark.

The presumption of civilisations is to prosper. The dream of our West is biodegradability, trying to be inconsequential.

While demanding our people progress in political and ideological terms, we laud the Australian Aborigines who lived without change for forty thousand years. Aside from a handful of stone huts in Victoria, they never constructed permanent dwellings. They slept in grass huts, under bark or tree branches, or in the open. Equating stability with sameness year after year, we call them in tune with their environment for leaving almost no evidence they'd been there. Romantically, perhaps truthfully, we accord them a philosophy that people should live and die leaving no record they'd been born.

We've adopted the mantra. Ours is the era when a West Australian politician was accused of racial vilification for calling Aborigines primitive. What we previously called primitive, we now call perfect.

No longer are we trying to sustain our civilisation: grand buildings and architecture, arts and culture. The generation after America landed on the moon no longer would, without a detailed environmental impact statement ensuring there'd be no footprints left behind.

We want no evidence of human presence, even a lowly turning of leaves on a forest floor. When Holyman Limited planned to deploy a ferry between the North and South Islands of New Zealand in 1994, seeing some of the most beautiful landforms and seashores on earth, the environmental impact study found the wash from the craft would disturb rocks on the seabed. It wouldn't break them, or mark them, but merely move them from one spot on the seabed to another. The proposed operator had the onus to prove the movement didn't constitute environmental damage.

We've come to conserve the natural environment oblivious to whether anyone enjoys it. People have nothing to do with it.

20. VOLUNTARY HUMAN EXTINCTION

"*We all want progress,*" wrote C.S. Lewis in *Mere Christianity*, "*but if you're on the wrong road, progress means doing an about-turn and walking back to the right road; in that case, the man who turns back soonest is the most progressive.*"

Put another way, Lewis is widely quoted to have said "When the whole world is running towards a cliff, he who is running in the opposite direction appears to have lost his mind." By the whole world, he should have said the West: Christian and not. The failings of the faithful don't cease without faith.

We're not going backwards if we resume a path the rest of the world never left. In what the West calls progress, we've regressed.

Among the little television I watched by May 2009 was part of a football game between Sydney and Port Adelaide. Late in the broadcast was an advertisement featuring actor Pierce Brosnan, who I'd first liked in the American television series *Remington Steele* and only liked more when he became James Bond in films. The advertisement called him a Man expert, whatever that meant. "There's more to life than making films," Brosnan said sultrily, "campaigning for the environment, finding time for myself."

They're the extremes of a white person's interests: the world on one hand and our individual selves on the other, without hint of anything beyond or between. The advertisement was for skincare, L'Oréal Expert Vita Lift. The only rival to the environment in importance to us is our skin.

Religious people bearing more children don't make the West warm to religion, not ours anyway. It's another reason to reject it.

"*As one of fifteen children,*" the *New Matilda* website said of Victorian senator Steve Fielding in 2009, "*he comes from a long line of people with no sense of human decency and so his affiliation with the Pentecostal movement was a natural progression.*" Fielding represented the Family First political party. *New Matilda* was founded by John Menadue, a former head of Australia's Department of Immigration. Large

Muslim families seem not to have bothered *New Matilda*.

New Matilda was positively respectful compared to the *Crikey* website, which set upon Fielding with its 'First Dog on The Moon' cartoon the last Thursday in June. It portrayed the senator being masturbated by Christ.

Fielding had raised their ire by trying to understand climate change theory. (Most people don't try to understand it. We just believe it.) Fielding didn't reject the theory, but wanted knowledge. Recognising differing points of view, he met with alarmists and sceptics, but scepticism is no longer a virtue. Fielding asked the Australian government to reply to the arguments of sceptics instead of fobbing them off.

Being a Christian of faith can only have complicated matters. Fielding thought about things, but our ideological orthodoxies can't comprehend questioning and investigating, at least not about anything important. Ideologies are our new Western sectarianism. All in all, the West imagines there'd be less conflict if Christianity and the rest of our cultures abated. Our people abating produce the same result.

By the first Tuesday of 2010, my friend Ian Biner had tired of wanting money and having little of it anyway. In the Rag & Famish bar, North Sydney, we talked of the world, and the West in which debate and discussion had given way to dogmas immersed in our destruction. He'd read enough to believe human activity had no impact upon climate, but referred to former American vice president Al Gore equating denial of global warming with denial of the Holocaust.

Gore wasn't Jewish. Media expert Ellen Goodman was. *"Let's just say that global warming deniers are now on a par with Holocaust deniers,"* she'd written in 2007, *"though one denies the past, and the other denies the present and future."*

"I'm sort of glad I don't have children," Ian told me, although circumstance rather than choice brought him there. "Western civilisation, the civilisation of the world, is collapsing."

That Ian, a secular Jew, should consider Western civilisation the civilisation of the world and care so much for its collapse said much about what Western civilisation had been, after all. When we'd worked together, our colleague the finance manager Peter said Ian often slipped into an American accent when speaking with Americans.

More often than not, climate change sceptics are people old enough to have witnessed the politicisation of knowledge, so we pay little credence to what we're told is a scientific consensus. We've seen scientific facts about race, gender, and sexuality replaced by ideologies masquerading as science. We've watched the world we've lived through replaced by an historical narrative unrelated to past reality. We've enough confidence in people, well some people at any rate, to know we can deal with changes to weather.

All sides agree climate changes. The West has lost confidence in our capacity to deal with it. Conversely, we're certain the weather is within our control, according ourselves the role we no longer give God. It's our arrogance to think we could save or destroy a planet. It's our despair to decide we're already destroying it.

When I long ago bought my Hard Rock Café sweater saying "*Save the Planet*," I thought the planet encompassed us. In Western minds, it no longer does.

"It's a planet!" I tell my children. "It's a whopping, great planet! It doesn't need saving."

Unlike other religions, our all-consuming Western environmentalism discourages childbearing. We have reason not just to stop growing, but to contract. Environmental concerns should cap immigration to ease environmental pressure, most obviously to California and the driest continent on earth, Australia, but that would be nationalist. Instead, we curtail births among us. "I've been a vegetarian for four years and I have chosen not to have children," American actor Vincent Kartheiser said in 2010, "which are both green choices in my life." Earlier that year, he'd said he didn't own a toilet.

We're martyrs in the best tradition of Christ. American weatherman Eric Holthaus responded to the 2013 report of the Intergovernmental Panel on Climate Change by deciding not to have children to reduce his carbon emissions. He considered a vasectomy. "*No children, happy to go extinct, which in and of itself, carries a certain sadness,*" he wrote on the Twitter website. A week earlier, Dutch artist and animal rights activist Tinkebell had herself sterilised for the same reason.

Intrinsic to our postmodern West is the same relentless sense within us: cowering to bleaker tones instead of what could be shining bliss. In spite of our bravado, central to our Western weak hearts lies hopelessness. There's hopelessness about the weather or our fixation with it, along with much more. Some of us try to improve things, but most feel we don't have a chance. Amidst all we call upon ourselves to bear, ours is the era no longer of war but futility.

Other races value their environments and fear climate change, but aren't sacrificing themselves to save us. When Islanders in low-lying South Pacific nations fear rising sea levels, they're saving themselves. Only the West thinks climate change is a reason to curtail childbearing. In spite of our low birth rate by 2007, obstetrics physician Barry Walters wanted the Australian government to charge parents with more than two children a baby levy for the carbon dioxide each child emitted, "in line with the 'polluter pays' principle."

People have become pollutants: toxins of an environment of which we're no longer a part. We complain that we consume mineral resources, as if they're not to be consumed. We've reduced our lives to the emission of carbon dioxide, denying animals oxygen while giving nothing they can't give. An earth filled with forests needs only animals to produce the carbon dioxide plants breathe. Fewer people mean more water for both. Environmental concerns that make us curtail populations of people don't make us curtail populations of pets.

Without racism, Western self-loathing becomes human self-loathing. If we're not lauding everyone else, we're damning us all. Our avowed globalism and self-hatred become a perfect storm. We no longer love nature because we love people, but because we despise them.

"We are a plague on the earth," said British environmentalist Sir David Attenborough in 2013. At least he spoke of limiting population growth in developing countries instead of only the West. "We keep putting on programmes about famine in Ethiopia; that's what's happening, too many people there. They can't support themselves, and it's not an inhuman thing to say. It's the case. Until humanity manages to sort itself out and get a co-ordinated view about the planet, it's going to get worse and worse."

He spoke the language of empire, but we're unwilling to control other populations. Other races aren't as prepared as we are fatalistically to fade, so we satisfy ourselves with the pleasure of letting us die.

The Voluntary Human Extinction Movement isn't willing to wait. The movement, as it calls itself, perceives human existence in terms of suffering. (Let's face it, meetings of most organisations can be tedious, but theirs must be horrific.) Blaming human beings for other species becoming extinct, it wants the earth returned to what it calls "*humanless splendour,*" wiping every person away.

That was the same humanless splendour from which dinosaurs and a whole bunch of other species became extinct before humans appeared. Species have constantly evolved and become extinct on this planet, quite apart from those variations of frog threatened with extinction when someone wants to build a road near a marsh. The only difference between them and our postmodern, multicultural, individualist West is the voluntariness of our demise. We hate human beings.

Less anyone doubt the Voluntary Human Extinction Movement is for European peoples, its website delivered its message in eighteen different languages, as of February 2012. Those languages didn't include languages of the most populous races on earth: Mandarin, Cantonese, or Hindi. Instead, they reached throughout Europe and the rest of the West, including countries of small populations and for good measure a region not a country: Belarusian, Catalan, Dutch, English, Finnish, French, German, Italian, Norwegian, Polish, Portuguese, Romanian, Russian, Slovenian, Spanish, and Swedish.

There'd been two languages added since I first checked the site in June 2008. Never did Israel or Turkey seem Western, until I saw Hebrew and Turkish there. Europeans might've been embracing them again.

Causes that could've valued people above all else have become corrupted into more ways of making people disappear. Only the West imagines purpose to a universe without us: our descendants to experience it. Instead of seeing paradise in nature encompassing our beautiful selves, Western environmentalism sees paradise without us: nirvana for no one to see. It comes not from respect for us, but contempt: not from belief in God giving us dominion over the earth to enjoy and protect, but rejection of us having dominion at all. Stripped of self-respect, we're less important than lichen.

We pursue oblivion to benefit animals, plants, and rocks, thinking we're worse than all the plagues God wreaked upon

Egypt, if we know anything of life before we were born. Saving the beetles and plankton, ours is human sacrifice: our own. Bugs and birds we yearn to save can break through our fading flesh as we've invited them to do, gnawing at the calluses we don't realise are ours.

The post-Christian West is sin without redemption, in spite of our best labours: sacrifice without resurrection. It's the earth in desperate darkness at the point of Christ's harrowing, cruel death: the curtain in the Temple torn. It's again waiting the news of that first Easter morning: the Resurrection and redemption.

Christian Europe valued human life in honour of God who granted us life. No longer believing in afterlife leaves people willing to lose the last life they have left. If there's reason in them not bearing children for the sake of the world, there's reason for them leaping straight to their deaths.

21. THE END OF CHRISTENDOM

The third Sunday of June 2013, the community minister at our family's Uniting church explained why the Asylum Seeker and Refugee Support Group (which accompanied the Amnesty International logo in the pew bulletins) would walk in support of asylum seekers the following Saturday. "We welcome everyone," she said, more assertively than she normally spoke, of not just our church but the West.

The community minister led the family connections ministry team; her husband also attended the church, when he was not travelling on church business. She certainly did welcome everyone. She had carried on the clandestine affair with the husband of her colleague, the children's minister, as I learnt seven years later. At least they were heterosexual.

Western churches make much of Christ's command to welcome a stranger from verse 35 onwards in the Gospel of Matthew, chapter 25, but it's among a litany of commands to help people in need. The stranger isn't simply someone seeking a better life. Verse 40 restricts the obligation to Christ's brethren: Christians.

Christ never says we should surrender our home or let our people suffer. After granting our hospitality, even shelter for the night, we should bid strangers on their way.

Instead, the cathedral at Nantes went so far as to employ an asylum seeker from Rwanda, who arrived in France in 2012. In 2020, France prepared to deport him, then thirty-nine years of age. In response, he set a fire that destroyed the cathedral organ built in 1621 and could have destroyed the six-hundred-year-old cathedral.

For a while there, I called this book *Saving Christendom* because Christendom can be saved. The first weeks of September 2015, the title again became *The End of Christendom*.

Initial news reports of two people brutally murdering two ordinary shoppers in an IKEA department store in Vasteras, Sweden the second Monday in August 2015 made no mention of race or religion. Two days later came news that Swedish police had responded to the unprovoked murders by boosting security not for Swedes but for asylum seekers, fearing they could be victims of a revenge attack. Only then we learned the murderers were two Eritrean asylum seekers. They'd beheaded two Swedish strangers in a store: a mother and her son.

Mainstream media didn't publish pictures of the victims alive or dead, or say very much about them. Instead, they published stock photographs of typical IKEA stores. Few and brief as reports of the murders were, they soon disappeared.

Yet news services repeated endlessly a photograph of Syrian boy Alan Kurdi washed up dead on the Turkey shore the second day of September 2015. The Syrian civil war had been under way for four years and millions of people settled in camps in adjoining countries, when Chancellor Angela Merkel seemed to suspend European Union rules requiring the countries where immigrants first arrive to process their asylum claims. She promised to accept all Syrian refugees reaching Germany, estimated to be a staggering eight hundred thousand before rising to more than a million that year alone.

Berlin tried to cut back Germany's promise, but tens of thousands of Arabs, Asians, and Africans were coming every day, with no sense they'd ever cease. "Germany! Germany!" they yelled, barging through Eastern Europe, overwhelming borders, laws, and people. "We want to go to Germany!"

Illegal immigrants, who normally dumped their identification papers before claiming asylum in the West, claimed to be Syrian. "I don't have a passport, nor any other identity paper," said Rafik from Pakistan, as he dashed under the fence into Hungary. (He'd given only his first name to avert repercussions applying for asylum in Germany.) "Let's see which country they will choose to kick me back to." European Union figures estimated that less than a fifth of the asylum seekers were Syrian.

Never before had a country or continent expressly invited invasion. (What other races call invasion, we call asylum.) This was no abstract situation. Here played out vividly before us was the end of Europe, over not decades but years or even weeks. The West's willingness since 1945 to give up our countries was being put to the test. We cried out that we were!

The first Monday evening that September 2015, Cath from our

family Uniting church was among thousands attending vigils for the masses swarming towards us. "I am a citizen of the world," she explained at our home group the following evening, a Tuesday, as to why she welcomed immigrants, whoever comes and however many.

"When we tell the world it's welcome, the world will come," I'd said.

"Good."

We welcome the world, come what may. Whiz (as she liked to be called, since her brother couldn't pronounce Elizabeth when he was small) didn't care that asylum seekers committed murders and other crimes like those in the IKEA department store a few weeks earlier. "White people do bad things too," she said. White children drown too, but that didn't diminish the West's response to a Syrian boy drowning.

We're willing to let white people suffer and die, to provide people of other races better lives. In effect, we're killing each other, claiming we're kind.

We have no thought of societies. Other races do.

Arab nations along the Persian Gulf enjoyed some of the world's highest incomes per capita. They spoke passionately about the Syrians' plight, some of them funding rebels in the Syrian civil war and giving money to aid refugees, but accepted only the workers they normally took. "You can't welcome people from another environment and another place who have psychological or nervous system problems or trauma and enter them into societies," explained Kuwaiti commentator Fahad Alshelaimi, of his fellow Muslim Arabs.

Saudi Arabia maintained a hundred thousand air-conditioned, fireproof tents eight kilometres from Mecca to accommodate three million people during the annual Haj. They lay empty the rest of the year. Its response to the refugees rushing into Europe was offering to build two hundred more mosques in Germany.

(Before the month was out came news that Saudi Arabia would become head of the United Nations Human Rights Council. It said less of human rights in Saudi Arabia than it said of the amoral United Nations' realpolitik.)

No news report I saw mentioned that Alan Kurdi had been living his three years of life safely in Turkey, before Germany's loud welcome enticed his family to board a boat to Greece that sunk. His father claimed the family had been refused refuge in Canada, which set off a storm of outrage among Canadians against their government, but the father never sought refuge there. He'd lied.

The boy's aunt living in Vancouver explained that the family hadn't sought asylum in Canada, because he needed dental work costing fourteen thousand dollars. Germany granted not just refuge, but also dental work.

When I told our Uniting church home group those details, Cath refused to believe them. When I told her that senator Cory Bernardi had mentioned them in his opposition to Australia increasing our refugee intake to accept more Syrians, she said she didn't believe anything Bernardi said.

As an example of asylum seekers lying, I listed the woman allegedly raped by Dominique Strauss-Kahn in 2011. Sometime earlier, her lies about being raped in Africa to get refugee status in America meant prosecutors believed Strauss-Kahn's lawyers could defeat her credibility as a witness. Still, Whiz rejected any criticism of asylum seekers. She criticised lawyers, pointedly at me.

We prefer Muslims to Christians. The only time I've heard anger from Whiz towards anyone I heard that night towards me for being white and rich (as if is the rest of us there weren't), but still wanting national borders to protect other white people. The only vitriol I've heard from James at our parish Anglican church is him berating white people he associates with nationalism. Nobody minds other races defending their countries.

The Archbishop of Canterbury, Justin Welby, had previously called Jesus a refugee, but Joseph and Mary weren't refugees in Bethlehem. They'd gone there to register for a census ordered by Caesar Augustus, according to the first verses of the Gospel of Luke, chapter 2. If not getting a room for the night makes someone a refugee, then my girlfriend and I were refugees in Epernay.

Equating Joseph, Mary, and Jesus fleeing the Massacre of the Innocents in Matthew, chapter 2, verse 14 with today's asylum seekers equates the murders of babies with not granting free dental care. It commoditises the Holy Family with thugs, vandals, and liars who reject Christianity. It's an affront to God.

The Holy Family returned to Judea when it was safe. Today's asylum seekers stay.

Unwilling to distinguish between different races and religions, Whiz equated the Muslim hordes entering Europe in 2015 to Jewish businessman Frank Lowy (her husband's ultimate boss for almost three decades). Born in Czechoslovakia, Lowy lived in Hungary during World War II before fighting for Israel and coming to Australia in 1952. He wasn't a refugee, but was of a race and religion not ours. That sufficed.

"*On a continent still haunted by World War II, ghostly – and ghastly – shadows of that convulsive conflict have been impossible to avoid as Europe grapples with its biggest refugee crisis since the war ended 70 years ago,*" wrote Henry Chu for the *Los Angeles Times* newspaper. When Hungary defended Europe by removing illegal immigrants from a train and detaining them in a camp in the town of Bicske, Austria's Chancellor Werner Faymann told Germany's *Der Spiegel* magazine that Hungary's policies were reminiscent of Nazism.

Middle Eastern refugees encapsulate the chains of Holocaust binding the West. The more millions of them we think we save, the more millions of Jews we feel we save. It will never be enough, because the Jews who died in the Holocaust are dead. No sacrifice now revives them.

Islamic terror drives us to defend not Christians but Muslims. Iranian cleric Man Haron Monis came to Australia as a political refugee. Eighteen years earlier, on the third Monday in December 2014, he held seventeen strangers hostage in the Lindt Chocolate Café, Martin Place, Sydney, forcing them to hold an Islamic flag at the window.

Two hostages, a mother of three young children and the café manager, died. Four hostages and a police officer were wounded. If the Sunni and Shi'ite Muslims reportedly blaming each other for the siege feared we'd think less of Muslims because of it, they need not have worried.

"*Australian Muslims!....,*" Father Bob Maguire declared through the *Twitter* website, "*mates....fear not....we have your back....you're not only Muslims but OUR Muslims....with respect, Auslims.*"

We welcome the persecuted and persecutors. Anything else would be discriminatory.

Among Australian churches calling for the country to accept more refugees, Gosford Anglican Church opposed any preference for Christians suffering persecution in the Middle East. "*No religious test for refugees,*" declared its public noticeboard, a photograph of which it published on the Facebook website and my friend James enthusiastically shared. *"'Christian' politicians suggesting that Christians should be given priority for refugee status show that they do not understand the essence of Christianity,"* claimed Father Rod Bower, *"nor do they truly appreciate the essence of secular democracy."*

His claim was nonsense, but in November 2017, Gosford Anglican Church's noticeboard declared: *"Christian lives don't matter. That's the whole point."* This was a suicidal church, trying to take the West with it.

When churches advocate secularism, we're denying our religion. We're denying Christians not special sanctuary, but any sanctuary.

The first Friday in October 2015, a fifteen-year-old boy shot dead a Chinese police accountant leaving Parramatta police headquarters, before shooting at police who shot him dead. Police said simply the murderer was a "radicalised youth of Middle Eastern background."

Initial *Australian Broadcasting Corporation News* reports omitted all hint of religion; he might have been a radical vegan. Later reports mentioned that he committed the murder after visiting a mosque. *"We must change the language about these tragedies and stop talking about religion and background,"* commented my friend James on Facebook. *"It does not help."*

The gunman, an Iranian with Australian citizenship, had wanted religion talked about. After the murder, he ran back and forth in front of police headquarters waving his gun in the air, shouting *"Allahu Akbar!"*

We're never fonder for the victims of crime and terrorism than when they're immigrants too, even if we define them not by their race but their job. *"The Police Family also lost a beloved brother, as did the Muslim Community,"* wrote Father Rod Bower. *"The N.S.W community lost two members, one who had already contributed much, the other's potential contribution denied us by a twisted manifestation of one of the world's great faith traditions."* Bower never wrote so glowingly of Christianity, as far as I saw.

Bower blamed us for the murder. *"We as a society have failed both the Cheng and Mohammad families."* God only knows what more we could have done, except leave them in their countries to start with.

The murderer had been a student at Arthur Phillip High School, where he attended voluntary lunchtime prayer sessions. A few months earlier, another student was suspected of preaching Islamic extremism during lunchtime prayer sessions at Epping Boys High School. With our refusal to differentiate between religions, within a week after the Parramatta murder came word that our youngest sons required parental permission to attend the Christian lunchtime gathering at our local high school. If schools prohibit Muslim meetings because of security concerns, they'll ban Christian ones too.

In October, messages such as *"convert or die"* and *"the caliphate is here"* covered the outside of Markus Samuelsson's bakery in Gothenburg, Sweden. Among was them was the Arabic letter N, used to identify homes of Christians in the Middle East whom Islamic State of Iraq and Syria wanted to drive out. Islamic State said it had sent four thousand fighters among the multitudes storming into Europe.

Immigrants rioted whenever East European countries obstructed their journeys to Germany, where German authorities evicted Germans from their homes to accommodate them. The last Wednesday of October, my friend James criticised those whose *"primary concern is the preservation of western civilisation and the protection of our way of life, it seems at the cost of others. How selfish and odd. Surely humanity matters more than disrupting our cosy way of life or preserving institutions."*

A few months earlier, James complained to me that Prime Minister Tony Abbott trashed Australia's institutions in response to Muslim terrorism. The institutions we defend to assist other races, we don't defend from them.

On New Year's Eve, mobs of immigrant men assaulted women in Germany, Austria, Switzerland, and Finland. In Berlin, they threw fireworks and fired guns, forcing women with prams to flee.

In the forecourt and on the steps of Cologne Cathedral, a thousand Arabs and North Africans threw bottles and exploding fireworks into groups of Germans, robbed them, sexually assaulted more than a hundred women, and pelted police vehicles with firecrackers. "I am Syrian," one told police. "You have to treat me kindly. Mrs Merkel invited me."

"You can't do anything to me," another told police, as he tore up his residence permit. "I can get a new one tomorrow."

Mainstream media didn't report the crimes until after several days of increasing social and then dissident media reports. German authorities insisted there was no evidence asylum seekers were involved, before *Die Welt* newspaper reported that in fact eighteen of thirty-one suspects identified by police were asylum seekers.

Lord Mayor Henriette Reker blamed the women, who "need to be better prepared…." Cologne City Council published guidelines advising them to stay at arm's length from strangers, remain within their group, and ask bystanders to intervene or act as witnesses. Reker expected Germans to educate people from "other cultures" as to acceptable conduct.

French satirical magazine *Charlie Hebdo* portrayed Alan Kurdi, had he not drowned, growing up to grope German women. The responsible artist, Laurent Sourisseau, a year earlier was wounded when Muslims attacked the *Charlie Hebdo* offices, murdering twelve people.

The first Thursday of March 2016, Pope Francis told a group of French Christians that Europe was undergoing an "Arab invasion," but that influxes of people enhanced Europe. Reminding us that our dream remains giving up the West into a single world civilisation, he'd just said that Europe is the only continent that can bring about a certain unity to the world." The only unity that Europe becoming Arab creates is with the Middle East, at Europe's expense.

Rarely does one monotheistic religion replace another, but Albania was Christian. Turkish colonisation and persecution made it Muslim.

Countries and even empires have undergone racial and religious transformations, most obviously Anatolia. Founded about 660 B.C., the Greek city of Byzantium became Constantinople and the eastern capital of the Roman Empire in 330: a centre of Christianity and Greek culture for a thousand years until the Ottoman Turks captured it in 1453 and the last of the Eastern Roman Empire fell. Multicultural along the way to being Muslim, the massive sixth-century St Sophia Church became a mosque, before the uneasy juxtaposition became the museum in which I stood a stranger in 1993.

In 2020, the museum became the Hagia Sophia mosque, to the cries of "*Allahu Akbar*!" We know the city as Istanbul, unaware it was ours.

The Greek and Roman cities of Troy lie in ruin, now in Turkey. At the beginning of the twentieth century, twenty percent of Turkey's population was Christian. A hundred years later, it's a hundredth of that.

The second Friday of April 2008, Palestinian Arab parliamentarian Yunis al-Astal delivered a sermon predicting the Muslim conquest of the West. "*They add the caveat 'Allah willing' to every threat,*" calmly commented Canadian Robert Vollman (a churchgoing Roman Catholic) on my friend Ian's website. "*So as long as Allah/God is unwilling to destroy his children, all their threats are empty. So on this technicality I'd say we're safe.*"

22. SAVING CHRISTENDOM

Most of us keep to our comfortable ecclesiastical corners with which we concur but early in the sixteenth century, for all the good deeds the Roman Catholic Church did, German priest Martin Luther took to task those in the Church who'd abandoned Scripture in favour of selling Papal indulgences. Today, for all the good deeds Western churches do (and several have been very good for me), Luther could chastise those corrupting Christianity in favour of multiculturalism, diversity, and other heresies.

We of the faith presume we don't need saving. We do. Christendom wanes, but will only end if we allow it. If we're not sitting idly by waiting for another Luther to rise and a sort of Reformation II, or Restoration, we'd better be Luther ourselves.

The second Friday evening of September 2015, while Western churches fell over themselves welcoming everyone to the West, I sat among a score or so worshippers in our parish Anglican church. We weren't there for aspiring invaders, but to remember thirty-five Australians who perished defending our country in His Majesty's Australian Submarine H.M.A.S. *AE1* in 1914. The organist, trumpeter, and I might have been the only people there not part of the small submariner community and their families.

Never before had I seen motorcycles parked outside the church, helmets on a table in the narthex, or members of a congregation wearing motorcycle jackets. Perhaps none of them normally attended church.

Father Keith spoke of the trauma our returned servicemen and women suffered coming home from Afghanistan and other wars to which we'd sent them, driving many of them to kill themselves. Keith, at his finest, offered his fellow former submariners seated before him his support at any time.

Whenever I read that month of Western political and church leaders offering their homes to Syrian families, as did the Archbishop of Canterbury at Lambeth Palace, I wondered how many homeless white people or white war veterans would have liked the same. If not cruelty, it's cruel neglect.

Beckoning them into Saint Peter's very seat of Christendom, Pope Francis offered to accommodate two Syrian families. The Vatican isn't a country. It's supposed to be a church.

Through recent years beforehand, Western countries had seen small and scattered but persistent protests against Islamisation of Europe and the West. September 2015, Western governments and churches thumbed their noses at those last expressions of Western nationalism, as if rapidly overwhelming those last loyalists with immigrants would force them to surrender.

Only East Europeans (who'd suffered the loss of their countries to another globalist ideology, Soviet communism) defended their peoples, countries, and Europe. "These migrants are not coming to us from war zones, but rather from camps in countries neighbouring Syria, like Lebanon, Jordan and Turkey," pointed out Hungary's Prime Minister Viktor Orban. "They were safe there." Immigrants weren't seeking asylum in Hungary, because they'd get better deals in Germany, Sweden, or Britain. Orban believed Europe would "perish" if she continued accepting millions of refugees.

Orban was a member of the Reformed Church in Hungary. His wife was Roman Catholic. Their love for God who gave us Jesus Christ, their country, and their people expressed the essence of Christianity, Christian nationalism, as I'd not seen or heard from leaders in Western Europe, the Americas, or Australasia for many years. Refusing to countenance Christians defending Christendom, the West stood ready to burn him at the stake.

The Czech Republic's President Milos Zeman called himself a "tolerant atheist," but still concluded his inaugural speech in 2013 with Christian prayer. He was a member of the Party of Civic Rights, which being East European included rights for her people. With the hordes storming into Europe in 2015, Zeman realised the children "serve as human shields for guys with iPhones to justify the wave of migrants... Those hiding behind the children...do not deserve any compassion." Jordan's Prince Zeid Ra'ad Al Hussein, the United Nations high commissioner for human rights, called him Islamophobic.

The Bible recognises that circumstances sometimes require Christians to fight. "*If it is possible, as far as it depends on you,*" wrote

Paul at chapter 12, verse 18 of his Epistle to the Romans, "*live at peace with everyone.*"

When foreigners threaten Europe in the twenty-first century, Western churches welcome them, but when Turkic peoples threatened Europe from the eleventh century, the Church sent Crusaders to defend us. The first of the Crusades began in 1095 under Pope Urban II. The last ended in 1272. The Crusades are typically the first answer to my question asking what wars religion caused, but as wars we now blame squarely upon Christians.

We're told the Crusades were unprovoked Christian aggression against peaceful Muslims at home. They weren't.

The Crusades were our response to Muslim Seljuk Turks from Persia conquering the Armenian capital in 1064 and the rest of Armenia in 1067. Turks conquered Jerusalem in 1065 where they massacred three thousand Christians, destroying churches or making them stables. Their defeat of Christian Europe at Manzikert in 1071 threatened the whole Byzantine Empire.

When Emperor Alexius I, a Greek, pleaded to his fellow Europeans for help, we didn't condemn his intolerance. We helped.

Franks were the most numerous of Crusaders, but the Crusades were a pan-European movement. They came from upper and lower classes in the commonality that race and religion were. Most Crusaders were men, some were women. Legend holds that in 1212, French and German children began Crusades. With piety and pilgrimage, we set forth to liberate European peoples.

Our ancestors were heroes and heroines. We're told they were villains.

On the second Thursday in March 2013, the *News Limited Network* responded to sixteenth-century French apothecary Nostradamus supposedly foreseeing that Francis I would be the last pope by listing several failed prophecies through history. (Now refusing to trust Jesus, the West blithely trusts Nostradamus.) The list focused upon erroneous Christians, including a prophecy I'd never before heard. "*The 1000th anniversary of the death of Jesus Christ was supposed to bring on Armageddon,*" said its website, of the year 1033. "*When it didn't happen, they launched the Crusades.*"

The journalist didn't know or care the Crusades occurred so many decades after 1033 or their real causes, possibly assuming a connection because they occurred in the same century. I typed my comment into the site pointing out the statement was untrue, but it was never published. No comments were.

The Crusades were a glorious failure. While we might know they failed, we're unaware of the Muslim invasions that inspired them. We're equally unaware that Muslims subsequently evicted Europeans from what became their land. (Had I not been researching this book, I wouldn't have known.) The Mamluks vowed to cleanse the Middle East of Franks, massacring or enslaving the last of them in 1291. It was much like Adolf Hitler trying to cleanse Europe of Jews, except the Mamluks succeeded.

Around about 1990, the Worldwide Evangelisation Crusade (at whose college my friend Bruce and his wife studied) changed its name to Worldwide Evangelisation for Christ because it feared talk of crusade rankled Arabs. Arabs reportedly did not care what happened eight hundred and more years ago in battles they ultimately won, until we cared so much.

By our rejection of Biblical Christianity and other Christian nationalism, we encourage and empower other races and religions with their nationalism. The rewritten Crusades make Muslim and that other Semitic immigration, the Jews, into Europe seem fair.

The Bible speaks to borders. Before nation states, there were city states, around which God allowed walls in their defence. Destruction of the walls, as occurred at Jericho (described in the Book of Joshua) represented the defeat and destruction of a people.

"Let us build up these towns," Asa said to Judah at chapter 14, verse 7 of the Second Book of Chronicles, "and put walls around them, with towers, gates and bars." So they built and prospered. At chapter 3 of the Book of Nehemiah, Nehemiah repaired the broken wall around Jerusalem.

Also asserting borders was the Roman Catholic Church, before multiculturalism. Following the sacking of the old St Peter's Basilica by Muslim Saracens in 846, Pope Leo IV commissioned the building of the Leonine Wall encircling Vatican Hill.

We did and thought all manner of things before multiculturalism, which we no longer do or think. Eighteenth-century Anglican cleric John Wesley, one of the forces behind Methodism, wrote that, "*ever since the religion of Mohammed appeared in the world, the espousers of it...have been as wolves and tigers to all other nations, rending and tearing all that fell into their merciless paws, and grinding them with their iron teeth; that numberless cities are raised from the foundation, and only their name remaining; that many countries, which were once as the garden of God, are now a desolate wilderness; and that so many once numerous and powerful nations vanished from the earth! Such was, and is at this day, the rage, the fury, the revenge, of these destroyers of human kind."*

God and Saint Peter entrusted Christianity to European peoples. Any church working against its people doesn't deserve to survive.

When Western Christians side with our races again rather than against them, we'll be churches again. When we stand again for Christian faith, embracing what God embraces and rejecting what He rejects, we'll be Christian again. We'll give people a reason to be Christian.

I believe Jesus Christ is the Son of God through essentially two streams of reasoning. The first is deductive, beginning with the universe and the extraordinary sophistication and complexity of life.

In 2014, psychological scientists Piercarlo Valdesolo and Jesse Graham reported in the journal *Psychological Science* that people seeing nature at its grandest are more likely than people in urban areas to pursue some understanding of the world. They become increasingly intolerant of uncertainty.

Our postmodern relativism compounds urbanisation, separating us from nature. Urbanisation compounds our relativism.

The more we experience the natural environment with people in mind, the more we believe in science and God. Believing God created everything is far more credible than thinking it simply arose or always was. God is the best explanation for its continuing as it does. Of all the theistic and polytheistic religions, the loving God that sent Jesus Christ I find the most credible.

The second stream of reasoning is inductive, beginning with the Nazarene Jesus. His Resurrection so convinced His Apostles and other followers that what He'd said through His ministry was true that they gave their lives to spread and defend the word of His divinity. History accords many inspirational people, but no other person inspired as He did. They honoured Him not because anyone compelled them, but in the face of every earthly persecution compelling them not to.

Atheism requires a greater leap of faith than does Christianity. Agnosticism is giving up without decision. Multiculturalism requires the greatest leap of faith of all, dismissing reams of historical and current evidence of religious and other cultural conflicts.

All nationalism requires is loyalty or practicality. Nationalism doesn't require love or Christian conviction, but love and Christian conviction command nationalism or other tribalism: taking precautions to protect our compatriots, making provisions to save our descendants. If Western individualists who sanctimoniously rejected racial and religious loyalty need people to protect them, they'll need to call upon white nationalists they despise.

"We are a world of nation states," said Malaysia's Prime Minister Najib Razak to the United Nations General Assembly the first day of October 2015, as other races but ours do. They are no citizens of the world. "Non-state actors, such as the so-called Islamic State, threaten to destroy sovereign states." (Islamic State sounded like Angela Merkel.)

Najib referred to Mohammed's command to Muslims to love one another, without thinking that meant loving non-Muslims. "This means there should be no strife among Muslims. Not between Shia and Sunni, who may take different paths, but seek the same destination." Mohammed commanded Muslim nationalism.

Christ commands Christian nationalism. "Love one another as I have loved you," He told His Disciples at chapter 13, verse 34 and at chapter 15, verse 12 of the Gospel of John.

He espoused nationalism in general. "If a kingdom is divided against itself," He said at chapter 3, verse 24 of the Gospel of Mark, "that kingdom cannot stand." The West is so divided, as are Western churches.

Christian expressions of goodness remain fine values for Christian communities, but only within Christian communities. Turning the other cheek when we suffer harm makes no sense towards self-serving individuals, other communities, and peoples of other religions.

Muslim, Christian, and Jewish nationalism are natural expressions of Islam, Christianity, and Judaism. Israel might have equated Muslim Syrians with Jews as far as Europe was concerned in 2015, but not as regards Israel. Its borders remained.

Nationalism doesn't mean we wantonly abandon our friends not of our race and religion. My friend Ian Biner's sense of being racially a Jew was absolute, defining him and uniting him with Jews across the world in their mutual defence and interests, but without the faith of his forebears let alone mine. He was a good son, who once wondered whether he and I should defer catching up one evening because his mother was serving Passover dinner that night. I told him we should defer, he should own his culture.

When Ian told his friends he'd developed leukaemia in February 2014, I telephoned him. Sometime through our brief conversation, I said spontaneously, as I could with Ian, "I'll pray for you."

In spite of my prayer, Ian died two weeks later. Again, I prayed. I prayed that Ian found faith in God through his final hours, but couldn't imagine he had. I prayed he'd had least found the faith of his forebears in the God of Abraham and Moses. I prayed that would bring him eternal life.

My last prayer was a prayer of intercession. In spite of Ian's likely failure to have realised Christ is the Son of God, I prayed that Christ and God would nevertheless bring him eternal life. I had no reason to think my prayer would prevail, and many a reason to know it would not. I wished for a universe in which Ian lived beyond death, but without him having found Christian faith, that isn't the universe. The universe doesn't change because we long for it to change.

Afterwards, praying for a Jew without his faith let alone mine sounded ridiculous. (No person I've known saw the absurdity of the world around us more clearly than did Ian.) I realised I pray for people because of God's relationship not with them, but with me. I pray for the West as much because of God's relationship with our forebears.

While ever enough of us survive to be a population, I'll pray that Western peoples recover our best sense of being races and nations: of being Christendom. Prayer compels us to do more than pray: to act, drawing upon whatever capacities God gives us. There'll be no great re-emergence of Western Christianity without Western Christians to lead it.

Our ancestors weren't willing to give up on us. Neither is God.

BIBLIOGRAPHY, REFERENCES

Articles

Adlam, Nigel, 'God helped them,' *NT News*, 20 September 2011.
Alexander, Sophie, "Convert or die' ISIS graffiti jihadis declare first European 'caliphate',' *The Daily Star* newspaper, 16 October 2015.
Aloisi, Silvia, 'Muslims more numerous than Catholics: Vatican,' *Reuters UK* news service, 30 March 2008.
Barrett, David, 'Christians have no right to wear cross at work, says Government,' *The Telegraph* newspaper, 10 March 2012.
Beck, Martha, 'Blinded by the Light?' *O, The Oprah Magazine*, May 2008. *Daily Lit* literature service *Oprah's Tips!*
Bibby, Paul, 'A time to celebrate – and enjoy peace and harmony,' *The Sydney Morning Herald* newspaper, 6 November 2011. Uncredited, '150 killed in Islamist attacks in Nigeria, *The Sydney Morning Herald* newspaper, 6 November 2011.
Bita, Natasha, 'Ban on naughty corner, easter egg hunts,' *The Australian* newspaper, 4 April 2011. Stephanie Klein, 'Seattle school renames Easter eggs 'Spring Spheres',' *My Northwest*, 7 April 2011. Uncredited, 'Ohio town is taking the 'Easter' out of its annual egg hunt,' *NBC 17 News*, 30 March 2011.
Blumberg, Antonia, 'Muslims Welcome: How One Australian Church Is Combating Islamophobia Amidst ISIS Outrage,' *The Huffington Post* website, 5 October 2014.
Brock, Parker, 'School system to get Muslim holiday,' *The Boston Globe* newspaper, 10 October 2010.
Bucci, Nino, 'Final Christmas message from Father Bob one of hope,' *The Age* newspaper, 26 December 2011. Uncredited, 'Father Bob gives final Christmas message,' *Australian Broadcasting Corporation News*, 25 December. Aleks Devic, 'Father Bob Maguire angry over witch hijacking wedding ceremony,' *Herald Sun* newspaper, 17 January 2012.
Campbell, Andy, 'The original Christmas story has echoes of the journey thousands face today,' *The Huffington Post* website, 25 December 2015.
Campion, Vikki, 'Last rites for English at Denistone East Uniting Church,' *The Daily Telegraph* newspaper, 15 March 2010.
Carney, Sean, 'Czech President Milos Zeman Casts Himself as

Unifier,' *The Wall Street Journal* newspaper, 8 March 2013. Sara Malm, 'Migrants are using children 'as human shields for men with iPhones' to justify arriving in Europe, says Czech Republic's president,' *Daily Mail* newspaper, 28 October 2015.

Chadwick, Father Anthony, "Game Over' for France, or will someone do something about it?' *The Anglo-Catholic (Catholic Faith and Anglican Patrimony)*, 9 January 2010.

Chesterton, Andrew, 'Coffins in Footy Team Colours Get the Nod,' *Sunday Telegraph* newspaper, 16 March 2008.

Chowdhry, Amit, 'Microsoft CEO Satya Nadella Apologizes For Comments On Women's Pay,' *Forbes Magazine*, 10 October 2014.

Collier, Myles, 'Christian Student Quits School Choir in Protest of Islamic Song,' *The Christian Post*, 16 February 2012. Uncredited, 'James Harper, Grand Junction High School Student, Quits Choir In Protest Over Plans To Sing Islamic Song 'Zikr',' *The Huffington Post* website, 15 February 2012.

Collins, Paul, 'ABC's mainstream religion tested, found wanting,' *Eureka Street* website published at *Crikey* website, 1 October 2009.

Costelloe, Kevin and Chiara Albanese, 'Pope Francis Refers To 'Arab Invasion' as a Social Reality,' *Bloomberg Business*, 5 March 2016, citing the Vatican newspaper *L'Osservatore Romano*.

Currie, Damien, 'Catholic Church says would-be brides are being too fussy,' *Herald Sun* newspaper, 7 May 2012. Lorissa's response was the second of the day to a summation of the article at *News Limited Network*.

Daily Mail reporter, 'Mother accused of murdering seven-year-old son for failing to learn the Koran made video confession days after,' *Daily Mail* newspaper, 14 November 2012.

Davies, Lizzy, 'Pope Francis completes contentious canonisation of Otranto martyrs,' *The Guardian* newspaper, 12 May 2013.

Day, Michael, 'Pope Francis assures atheists: You don't have to believe in God to go to heaven,' *The Independent* newspaper, 11 September 2013.

Devine, Miranda, 'Fielding changes Canberra's climate,' *The Sydney Morning Herald* newspaper, 13 June 2009, quoting the *New Matilda* website.

DeWitt, Jason, 'Muslims Demand That 'Offensive' Crosses Be Removed…From CATHOLIC School,' *Top Right News*, 16 May

2015.

Dillon, Jenny, 'Father-of-six Ron Williams will go to the High Court over religious classes in schools,' *The Daily Telegraph* newspaper, 26 January 2011.

Dinsdale, Margaret, 'Retired Scottish primus rethinks authority,' *Anglican Journal* newspaper, 1 April 2001.

Doherty, Elissa, 'Saint Nick sacked from Victorian pre-school so not to offend religious groups,' *Herald Sun* newspaper, 8 December 2010.

Donnelly, Kevin, 'All cultures and religions are not created equal,' *News Weekly*, July 2010.

Dudley, Renee, 'Cancer center's Santa gets boot,' *The Post and Courier* newspaper (Charleston, South Carolina), 16 November 2011.

Edwards, Steven, 'UN document would give 'Mother Earth' same rights as humans,' *Postmedia News*, 11 April 2011.

Eilperin, Juliet, 'Cancun talks start with a call to the gods,' *The Washington Post* newspaper, 29 November 2010.

Evans, Terry, 'Chase orders Southlake bank to remove Christmas tree,' *The Star-Telegram* newspaper, 2 December 2010.

Fife-Yeomans, Janet and others, 'Parramatta shooting: Multiple shots fired outside police HQ on Charles Street,' *The Daily Telegraph* newspaper, 3 October 2015. Uncredited, 'Gunman who shot dead NSW police employee was radicalised youth,' *Australian Broadcasting Corporation News*, 3 October 2015. Rachel Olding and Ava Benny-Morrison, 'Police probe teen gunman's school connections and group spreading Islamic State ideology,' *The Sydney Morning Herald* newspaper, 6 October 2015. Sarah Gerathy and staff, 'NSW school prayer audit completed amid concerns of extremist Islamic preaching,' *Australian Broadcasting Corporation News*, 8 October 2015.

Franklin, Matthew and Nicola Berkovic, 'Lindsay Tanner finds praise for school that beat him,' *The Australian* newspaper, 21 November 2008. Tanner's 2008 Redmond Barry Lecture was published at the *State Library of Victoria* website.

Goldman, Russell, 'Iowa Town Renames Good Friday to 'Spring Holiday',' *Australian Broadcasting Corporation News*, 29 March 2010.

Goodman, Ellen, 'No change in political climate,' *The Boston Globe* newspaper, 9 February 2007.

Gray, Louise, 'David Attenborough – Humans are plague on Earth,' *The Telegraph* newspaper, 22 January 2013.
Hassett, Sebastian, 'Talented young striker faces uncertain future after court charges,' *The Sydney Morning Herald* newspaper, 20 November 2010.
Hurst, Daniel, 'Father Kennedy's final St Mary's service,' *The Brisbane Times* newspaper, 19 April 2009.
Jaensch, Dean, 'Thou shalt separate Church and State,' *The Punch* website, 26 May 2011. I commented as Simon of Sydney.
Jensen, Robert, 'No Thanks for Thanksgiving,' *Alternet*, 21 November 2012.
Kelly, Jen, 'Baby tax needed to save planet, says WA expert,' *The Advertiser* newspaper, 10 December 2007, quoting Barry Walters in the *Medical Journal of Australia*.
Kern, Soeren, 'German Church Becomes Mosque: 'The New Normal',' *Gatestone Institute*, 12 February 2013. Uncredited, 'Mosques 'a feature of German landscape',' *The Sydney Morning Herald* newspaper, 18 September 2010, quoting Angela Merkel in the Frankfurter *Allgemeine Zeitung*.
Kettell, Steven, 'State Religion and Freedom: A Comparative Analysis,' *Journal of the Religion and Politics Section of the American Political Science Association* at *Cambridge Journals Politics and Religion*, 5 April 2013. Elizabeth O'Casey, 'Where there is state religion, there is less freedom,' *National Secular Society*, 4 April 2013.
Knox, Malcolm, 'Altar egos,' *The Sydney Morning Herald* newspaper, 6 November 2010, quoting Edmund Burke.
Lampathakis, Paul, 'Row over tennis legend Margaret Court's view that homosexuality is often the result of sexual abuse,' *The Sunday Mail* newspaper, 29 January 2012.
Lane, Oliver, 'Berlin, Cologne, Hamburg, Stuttgart, Dusseldorf… New Year's Migrant Sex Assault In Every Major German City,' *Breitbart London News*, 6 January, 2016. Oliver Lane, 'Cologne Mayor: Women Should Be More Careful After Migrant Mass Rapes, Promises 'Guidance' So They Can 'Prepare',' *Breitbart London News*, 5 January, 2016. Telegraph foreign staff, 'Mayor of Cologne condemned for urging women to 'keep men at arm's length' in new code of conduct to prevent assaults,' *The Telegraph* newspaper, 6 January 2016. Justin Huggler, 'Suspects in Cologne sex attacks 'claimed to be Syrian refugees',' *The Telegraph* newspaper, 7 January 2016. Subsequent reports

numbered the women assaulted in Cologne at more than a hundred. Network writer, 'New Year's Eve sex assaults also reported in Finland, Sweden and Austria,' *Agence France-Presse* news service published on the *News Corp Australia Network*, 8 January 2016, which referred to Switzerland, not Sweden.

Lane, Oliver, 'Latvia An Islamic State In 50 Years, Boast Muslim Community Leaders, 'Integration Will Not Take Place',' *Breitbart News*, 15 October 2015.

Lefkovits, Etgar and Rebecca Anna Stoil, 'Pope under fire for Yad Vashem speech,' *The Jerusalem Post* newspaper, 11 May 2009.

Llana, Sara Miller, 'Sweden tries something new for annual Christmas TV special: a Muslim host,' *The Christian Science Monitor*, 23 December 2015.

Lutton, Phil, 'Cash demand may be extortion,' *The Sydney Morning Herald* newspaper, 14 June 2012. Uncredited, 'London 2012 Olympics: Australian weightlifter Daniel Koum 'held federation to ransom' over pre-Games event,' *The Telegraph* newspaper, 13 June 2012.

Mail Online reporter and Associated Press, 'Immigration official mother of Canadian gunman reveals they were reunited last week after five year estrangement but has 'no explanation' for his terrorist conversion,' *Daily Mail* newspaper, 23 October 2014.

Marriner, Cosima, 'God may be first casualty as Guides look for a fresh start,' *The Sydney Morning Herald* newspaper, 6 November 2011.

Marszalek, Jessica, 'School sorry for refusing Sikh student,' *Australian Associated Press* news service, 2 September 2008.

McKenny, Leesha, 'Gay ministers show a Uniting front to lead congregations, *The Sydney Morning Herald* newspaper, 22 August 2011.

McKenny, Leesha, 'Ramadan shakes off retail gloom with a festive finish,' *The Sydney Morning Herald* newspaper, 18 August 2011.

McNeilage, Amy, 'Ramadan brings different cultures to the table,' *The Sydney Morning Herald* newspaper, 12 August 2012.

O'Brien, Susie, 'Schools steer clear of Christmas,' *Herald Sun* newspaper, 16 December 2011.

Olson, Marie-louise, "No children, happy to go extinct', tweets weatherman after grim climate-change report made him cry (now he's considering a vasectomy),' *Daily Mail* newspaper, 28

September 2013.
Opelka, Mike, 'Anti-Christian Hate Speech Spews From The Palm Beach Dem Chair,' *The Blaze*, 5 September 2012.
Petchers, Stephanie, 'Ibtihaj Muhammad, Team USA's First Olympian To Wear A Hijab, Is Winning Hearts Everywhere,' Huffpost Video, *The Huffington Post* website, 10 August 2016.
Petersen, Hayley, 'Missouri pastor stuns local politicians with shocking twist to his argument against equal rights for homosexuals,' *The Mail on Sunday* newspaper, 21 October 2012.
Schorr, Rebecca Einstein, 'Goy: Origin, Usage, and Empowering White Supremacists,' *Forward* website, 21 August, 2017.
Sharwood, Anthony, 'A football field is no place for nutty religious fanaticism,' *The Punch* website, 17 January 2012.
Sharwood, Anthony, 'Imam dreaming of a fatwa Christmas,' *The Punch* website, 23 December 2012. Andy's comment was published at 1.37pm. Natalie O'Brien, 'No merriness here: mosque puts fatwa on Christmas,' *The Sydney Morning Herald* newspaper, 23 December 2012. Rachel Olding and Natalie O'Brien, 'Outrage over 'fatwa' forces mosque to pull down website post,' *The Sydney Morning Herald* newspaper, 24 December 2012.
Shaviv, Miriam, 'Candidate Ken's attitude to Jews may be key in race to run London,' *Jewish Times* newspaper, 27 April 2012. Ken Livingstone's interview with Leslie Bunder, *Something Jewish* website, 17 November 2005.
Shuster, Simon, 'Why Refugees From Old Wars Are Only Rushing To Europe Now,' *Time* magazine, 4 September 2015. Ben Hubbard, 'Wealthy Gulf Nations Are Criticized for Tepid Response to Syrian Refugee Crisis,' *The New York Times* newspaper, 5 September 2015. Stojanovic Dusan, 'Migrants in the Balkans: Everyone wants to be Syrian,' *Associated Press* published in *The Sydney Morning Herald* newspaper, 6 September 2015. Boethius, 'Reality Check,' *XYZ* website, 6 September 2015. Henry Chu, 'Europe's refugee crisis is darkened by the shadows of WWII,' *Los Angeles Times* newspaper, 5 September 2015. Barbara Miller with *Reuters* news service, 'European migrant crisis: Hungary hits back at Austria's criticism of 'Nazi-like' asylum seeker policies,' *Australian Broadcasting Corporation News*, 13 September 2015. Jake Burman, 'Just ONE IN FIVE migrants claiming asylum are from Syria, EU figures show,'

Daily Express newspaper, 19 September 2015. Uncredited, 'Archbishop of Canterbury offers cottage to refugees,' *BBC News*, 20 September 2015.

Sinco Kelleher, Jennifer, 'Not all born in American Samoa want US citizenship,' *Associated Press* news service, 9 February 2020, quoting Charles Ala'ilima and Tisa Fa'amuli.

Spencer, Robert, 'Sweden: Court rules that employers must pay Muslims for praying on the job,' *Jihad Watch*, 21 September 2020.

Starnes, Todd, 'University Takes Action to Punish Student,' *Fox News & Commentary* at *News Radio 1200 WOAI* in San Antonio, Texas, 25 March 2013.

Street, Jon, 'Muslim Parent Warns School Board 'We're Going to Be the Majority Soon' as Meeting Gets Heated and Security Is Needed,' *The Blaze*, 22 September 2015.

Stringer, David with Raphael Satter, 'Iran leader's Christmas message decries bullies,' *Associated Press* news service, 24 December 2008. Liz Thomas, 'Outrage as Channel 4 lets Iranian ruler give 'offensive' alternative Christmas message,' *Daily Mail* newspaper, 26 December 2008.

Syson, Neil, 'Sheikh flies his Lamborghini for service from Qatar to London,' *The Sun* newspaper, 31 July 2008.

Tapscott, Mark, 'Congressmen can't say 'Merry Christmas' in mail,' *The Washington Examiner* newspaper, 16 December, 2011.

Thornhill, Ted, 'How the Grand Canyon makes us religious: Natural wonders increase our tendency to believe in God and the supernatural,' *Daily Mail* newspaper, 26 November 2013.

Uncredited, '3 Columbus churches vandalized with graffiti overnight,' *WTHR Channel 13 Indiana*, 1 September 2014.

Uncredited, 'Ancient prophecies point to Pope Francis being the last,' *The Courier Mail* newspaper, 14 March 2013.

Uncredited, 'Christians versus Fairies,' *The Australian* newspaper, 11 August 2007.

Uncredited, 'Couple kept sham marriage to stop violent reprisals,' *The Sydney Morning Herald* newspaper, 31 July 2010.

Uncredited, 'Feds Force Okla. Bank to Remove Crosses, Bible Verse,' *KOCO Television*, Oklahoma, 16 December 2010. Uncredited, 'Lawmakers Call Out Bernanke After Feds Force Bank To Remove Crosses,' and 'After Outcry, Feds Back Down; Banks Can Display Crosses,' *KOCO Television*,

Oklahoma, 17 December 2010.

Uncredited, 'File sharing as religious community in Sweden,' *The Sydney Morning Herald* newspaper, 6 January 2012.

Uncredited, 'Five decades of service ends,' *The Age* newspaper, 26 May 2003, concerning Peter Hollingworth.

Uncredited, 'Football fans executed for watching World Cup,' *The Telegraph* newspaper published in *The Sydney Morning Herald* newspaper, 15 June 2010.

Uncredited, 'French scarf ban comes into force,' *BBC News*, 2 September 2004.

Uncredited, 'Ga. Seniors Told They Can't Pray Before Meals,' *The Associated Press* news service, 8 May 2010.

Uncredited, 'Gaddafi's religious gaffe,' *Agence France-Presse, Bloomberg* news services published in *The Sydney Morning Herald* newspaper, 1 September 2010. Gaddafi didn't consider his words a gaffe.

Uncredited, 'Gay nativity scene vandalized at Claremont church,' *Los Angeles Times* newspaper, 29 December 2011.

Uncredited, 'Malaysian court rules use of 'Allah' exclusive to Muslims,' *Reuters* news service published at *Australian Broadcasting Corporation News*, 14 October 2013. Niluksi Koswanage, 'Malaysia's Islamic authorities seize Bibles as Allah row deepens,' *Reuters* news service, 2 January 2014.

Uncredited, 'Pakistani model dead after offending conservatives,' *The Associated Press* news service published at *CBS News*, 16 July 2016.

Uncredited, 'Prosecutors reveal DSK's 'brief' sex with maid probably not consensual but she repeatedly lied,' *Agence France-Presse* news service published in *The Sydney Morning Herald* newspaper, 23 August 2011.

Uncredited, 'Rosaries, ovaries T-shirt 'not vilification',' *Australian Associated Press* news service, 4 December 2006.

Uncredited, 'Student reportedly suspended after saying 'Bless you',' *WMC Action News 5*, 20 August 2014.

Uncredited, 'Sweden boosts security for asylum seekers after IKEA knife attack; two Eritrean suspects detained,' *Reuters* and *Agence France-Presse* news services published at *Australian Broadcasting News*, 12 August 2015. Australian Broadcasting Corporation and wires, 'IKEA knife attack: Two killed, one injured in Sweden home store,' *Australian Broadcasting News*, 11 August 2015. Michael Miller, 'In Sweden's Ikea attack, two migrants, two slayings and rampant fear of refugees,' *The Washington Post* newspaper, 29 September 2015.

Uncredited, 'Tips and rumours: God be with you, NSW A-G urges,' *Crikey* daily mail, 22 December 2011.

Uncredited, 'UK students taught how to chop off hands: BBC,' *Agence France-Presse* news service published at *The Sydney Morning Herald* newspaper, 22 November 2010.

Uncredited, 'Vincent Kartheiser: I Won't Have Kids for Environmental Reasons,' *The Huffington Post* website, 17 November 2010.

Uncredited, 'Woman charged with vandalism had can with green paint,' *WTOP* and *Associated Press* news service, 31 July 2013.

United States Holocaust Memorial Museum, 'German Churches and the Nazi State,' *Holocaust Encyclopedia*.

Valdesolo, Piercarlo and Jesse Graham, 'Awe, Uncertainty, and Agency Detection,' *Psychological Science* journal, January 2014.

Wardill, Steven, 'Tree costing taxpayers millions,' *The Courier Mail* newspaper, 20 May 2008.

Watts, John, 'Faith not for streets,' Letters to the Editor, *The Sydney Morning Herald* newspaper, 5 September 2011.

Wrobleski, Tom, 'Baby Jesus ousted from St. George Ferry Terminal,' *Staten Island Live*, 10 December 2010.

Zwartz, Barney, 'Compensate Aborigines or leave, says minister,' *The Sydney Morning Herald* newspaper, 11 August 2009.

Zwartz, Barney and Peter Cai, 'Asian followers give life to Christian churches,' *The Sydney Morning Herald* newspaper, 9 April 2012.

Books and Letters

Ali, Ayaan Hirsi, born 1969, *Nomad: From Islam to America: A Personal Journey Through the Clash of Civilizations* (2010), Free Press. Rebecca Weisser, 'Hirsi Ali urges refugee testing,' *The Australian* newspaper, 26 July 2010. Heather Tyler, 'Christianity can combat conservative Islam threat,' *The Daily Telegraph* newspaper, 30 July 2010.

Cammaerts, Émile, 1878-1953, *The Laughing Prophet* (1937), a Belgian poet, discussing the story 'The Oracle of the Dog' in *The Incredulity of Father Brown* (1926), might be the author of the words widely attributed to English writer G K Chesterton,

1874-1936: "People no longer believing in God don't believe in nothing, but in everything."

God, eternity, The Bible (various dates, a long time ago), New International Version.

Hobson, Theo, born 1972, *Against Establishment: An Anglican Polemic.* Theo Hobson, 'Liberal guilt is nothing for a decent society to be ashamed of,' *The Guardian* newspaper in *The Sydney Morning Herald* newspaper, 31 August 2010.

Kaufmann, Eric, *Shall the Religious Inherit the Earth: Demography and Politics in the Twenty-First Century* (2010), Profile Books. Eric Kaufmann, 'Out of mouths of babes – religious will rise as secular birth rates fall,' *The Sydney Morning Herald* newspaper, 20 September 2010.

Lewis, C S, 1898-1963, *Mere Christianity* (1952).

Lingel, Joshua and others (editors), *Chrislam: How Missionaries Are Promoting an Islamised Gospel.* Joel Richardson, 'New Bible Yanks 'Father,' Jesus As 'Son Of God',' *World Net Daily*, 30 January 2012.

Marx, Karl, 1818-1883, *Contribution to the Critique of Hegel's Philosophy of Right* (written 1843, introduction published 1844, remainder published after Marx's death).

Miller, John, *All Them Cornfields and Ballet in the Evening* (2010). Page 180 described the funeral of Leonid Brezhnev.

Muggeridge, Malcolm, 1903-1990, *The End of Christendom* (1980).

Murphy, John Patrick Michael, *The Religion of Hitler* (1998).

Putnam, Robert and David Campbell, *American Grace: How Religion Unites and Divides Us* (2011). Chaeyoon Lim and Robert Putnam, 'Religion, Social Networks, and Life Satisfaction,' *American Sociological Review* journal, December 2010. Daily Mail reporter, 'Going to church makes you happy: Religion affirms sense of belonging,' *Daily Mail* newspaper, 7 December 2010. Simon Smart, 'God's truth, believers are nicer,' *The Sydney Morning Herald* newspaper, 9 September 2011, citing the 2004 report by the Department of Families, Community Services and Indigenous Affairs, *Research and Philanthropy in Australia.*

Voltaire, born François-Marie Arouet, 1694-1778, letter to the author of the book *The Three Impostors* (1770).

Wesley, John, 1703-1791, *The Works of the Reverend John Wesley A.M.*, edited by John Emory (1831), especially page 508.

Cantatas

Son of David.

Documentaries

In Bob We Trust (2013).
Life of Jesus (2009) narrated by John Dickson, Centre for Public Christianity. During the conversation titled 'Could God really become a man?' was pictured the banner quoting the Koran near the Church of the Annunciation in Nazareth.

Films

2012 (2009), written by Harald Kloser and Roland Emmerich. Tracy Connor and Maureen Mullen, 'Newtown, Mayan end-of-world rumors prompt Michigan officials to close 33 schools,' *NBC News*, 20 December 2012.
Gandhi (1982), written by John Briley.
Ghostbusters (1984), written by Dan Aykroyd and Harold Ramis, originally called *Ghost Busters*. Now, there's a profound change.
Noah (2014), written by Darren Aronofsky and Ari Handel. Barbara Nicolosi, 'Noah – The Emperor's New Movie,' *Church of the Masses*, 27 March 2014.
Passion of the Christ, The (2004), written by Mel Gibson and Benedict Fitzgerald, directed by Mel Gibson.
Square, The (2008), written by Joel Edgerton and Matthew Dabner.

Hymns

'All Things Bright and Beautiful.'

Judgments

Abington School District v Schempp, 374 U.S. 203 (1963).
Goodridge v Dept. of Public Health, 798 N.E.2d 941 (Mass. 2003). Sam De Brito, 'That doesn't sound very Christian to me,' *The Sydney Morning Herald* newspaper, 26 November 2013.

Parliamentary Reports

Australian Parliamentary Hansard, 12 November 2008, Melissa Parke eulogising the late Keith Dowding.

Songs

'I Saw Momma Kissing Santa Claus' (1952), words and lyrics by Tommie Connor, 1904-1993.
'Jingle Bells' (1857, in its original form), by James Lord Pierpont, 1822-1893.
'Rudolph the Red Nosed Reindeer' (1939) by Johnny Marks, based upon a story of that name by his brother-in-law Robert May, 1905-1976, both Jews.
'Santa Claus is Coming to Town' or 'Santa Claus Is Comin' to Town' (1934), written by John Frederick Coots, 1897-1985, and James "Haven" Lamont Gillespie, 1888-1975.
'YMCA' (1978), sung by the Village People. No, really, it was.

Television Programmes

All Creatures Great and Small (1978-1990). Peter Davison played Tristan Farnon.
Doctor Who (1963-1989, 2005 onward). Peter Davison was one of many actors who played the Doctor.
Hidden Story of Jesus, The (2007).
M*A*S*H (1972-1983).
Network (13 August 2007). Radio Netherlands, 'Dutch bishop says Christians should call God 'Allah',' *Catholic News Agency*, 15 August 2007.
Remington Steele (1982-1987).

ABOUT THE AUTHOR

Simon Lennon has travelled throughout Europe, America, Australasia, Asia, and the South Pacific, seeing how similar European peoples are to each other (wherever we live) and how different we of the West are to everyone else. He has university bachelor's degrees in science and law and university master's degrees in commerce and business. He is married with six children.

His non-fiction collection *The West* comprises the following sixteen books:

Mending the West
The Unnatural West: An Overview
The Tribeless West: An Overview
The Homeless West: An Overview
The Vanishing West: An Overview

Individualism
Western Individualism
The End of Natural Selection
The Need for Nations

Identity
People's Identity: Race and Racism
Of Whom We're Born: Race and Family
Biological Us: Gender and Sexuality

Nationalism
A Land to Belong: Nationalism
The Failure of Multiculturalism

Cultures
Reclaiming Western Cultures
Christendom Lost
Aiding Islam

He is also the author of another non-fiction book, two collections of short stories, and five novels.

www.ingramcontent.com/pod-product-compliance
Lightning Source LLC
LaVergne TN
LVHW041620070426
835507LV00008B/368